PELICAN BOOKS
A452

THE IDEA OF THE HOLY

RUDOLF OTTO

The Idea of the Holy

RUDOLF OTTO

Translated by
JOHN W. HARVEY

PENGUIN BOOKS

Penguin Books, Ltd, Harmondsworth, Middlesex
AUSTRALIA: Penguin Books Pty Ltd, 762 Whitehorse Road,
Mitcham, Victoria

—

First published 1917
English translation published in Great Britain by Oxford University Press 1923
Published in Pelican Books 1959

Made and printed in Great Britain
by Unwin Brothers Limited
Woking and London

CONTENTS

Contents

DEDICATED TO
THEODOR VON HÄRING

NOTE ON TRANSLATION AND APPENDIX

THIS translation was originally made from the ninth German edition of *Das Heilige*. 'The Expression of the Numinous in English' was added by the translator. Additions to the text at the close of Chapters 6 and 11 were added in 1928 from the fourteenth German edition.

OTHER WORKS OF RUDOLF OTTO TRANSLATED INTO ENGLISH ARE

NATURALISM AND RELIGION
Translated by J. Arthur Thomson and Mildred R. Thomson
London (Williams and Norgate), 1907

INDIA'S RELIGION OF GRACE
Translated by F. H. Foster
London (S.C.M. Press), 1930

THE KINGDOM OF GOD AND THE SON OF MAN
A Study in the History of Religion
Translated by Floyd V. Filson and B. Lee Woolf
London (Lutterworth Press), 1930

RELIGIOUS ESSAYS
A Supplement to the Idea of the Holy
Translated by L. B. Dicker (with a Foreword by W. Tudor Jones)
London (Williams and Norgate), 1931

MYSTICISM EAST AND WEST
A Comparative Analysis of the Nature of Mysticism
Translated by Bertha L. Bracy and Richenda C. Payne
London (Macmillan), 1932

THE ORIGINAL GITA
The Song of the Supreme Exalted One with copious comments and notes by Rudolf Otto
Translated and edited by J. E. Turner
London (Allen and Unwin), 1939

INTRODUCTION

WHEN Rudolf Otto wrote *Das Heilige* in 1917, he held a professorship of Theology in the University of Marburg, which since the beginning of the century had had a high reputation for both theological and philosophical learning. But he was not an exponent of any of the typical interests of Theology as it was then taught either in Germany or in England. He was neither concerned to expound traditional dogmas of Christian orthodoxy, nor to defend them against heresies, nor to subject them to drastic criticism or fundamental restatement. Nor had he any deep interest in tracing and interpreting the course of Church History, nor yet again was he a profound textual critic of the Scriptures. It was in fact rather the Philosophy of Religion than Theology that formed his main interest; yet this too may be misleading. For one type of 'religious philosophy' is occupied with the endeavour to justify (or, it may be, to refute) the claim of a religion to be taken seriously, but to do so on rational grounds – to show that the religious point of view is essentially a *reasonable* one; whereas Otto, as this, his chief book, makes defiantly clear, is concerned to show that though the religious view of the world is indeed 'reasonable', this is only because it is 'reasonable' to recognize that experience brings us to confront a Reality that is not *merely* to be rationally apprehended, because it extends beyond the compass of any purely rational faculty, but is yet not outside experience altogether.

What is involved in Religion as a human *experience*? That question may well suggest to an English reader the title and content of William James's famous lectures on *The Varieties of Religious Experience* (1902). Certainly James, like Otto, took religion seriously; he was perhaps the first professional psychologist to write of it with a really lively insight and sympathy. But in two respects his approach to the subject was in sharp contrast to that of Otto fifteen years later. First, James was, as the title of his book indicates, specially interested in the diversities of religious experience, whereas Otto, while recognizing the diversities, is much more concerned to bring out essential common elements which all religions exemplify though some much more adequately

9

than others. For him, even strange aberrations are indicative of the true apprehension which they may grotesquely mis-represent. His treatment of evidences may lack James's vivacious exuberance but it is no less penetrating. And he had a far wider and deeper first-hand knowledge both of the great religions of the East, in China, Japan, and especially in India, and of savage cults in which for all their crudity or cruelty he found adumbrations of something august. He had travelled widely, in America and the Far East as well as (historically) back through the centuries.

The other respect in which the points of view of James and Otto are in sharp contrast is of more crucial importance towards the understanding of this book. James was a psycho-logist, and as such very much interested in *states of mind*. 'Feelings' mean for him stirrings of emotion, such as fear, self-disgust, confidence, or rapture. But the 'feelings' with which Otto is concerned are nearly always, as philosophers would put it, objective in their reference; they point out-wards not inwards; they are the reaction in a man to some apprehension of a reality beyond himself, which *affects* him, and it is the clue to that reality given by the 'affect' which Otto is seeking to follow up. The reader of this book should use the term *feeling* more in the sense in which we say 'I am sure I feel there is someone watching me' than in the sense of 'I feel unhappy' or 'contented'. The 'feelings' Otto has to explore are, he seeks to show, though a *non*-rational sort of apprehension, in no sense an *anti*-rational element in human experience. In religion at its highest the rational and non-rational are (in a favourite metaphor) intimately 'woven together'.

This experiential mode of religious inquiry, drawing not only in ample measure upon the sacred texts and teachings of the high religions but upon the findings of anthropo-logists concerning what might well be called the peculiarities of primitive experience, certainly marked the opening of a new chapter in German religious thinking, and the signi-ficance of Otto's work has been recognized likewise in other countries. He would none the less have been the first to admit, or rather to claim, that his thought owed much to German philosophical theology of the past.

If in his approach to the interpretation of Religion Otto was quite unlike his older contemporaries and immediate predecessors in the field of theology and religious philosophy, his personality and general outlook upon life were equally uncharacteristic of the German academic scholar and teacher, at any rate as so commonly presented. He was no self-isolated *Gelehrter*, immersed in his studies, uninterested in the world about him, or in other people. He was on the contrary particularly eager to share his thoughts with others and to learn from them; a most friendly companion, a patient listener, and a man of wide and varied sympathies. And he had the sort of humour which Englishmen like to think of as peculiar to them; he certainly enjoyed English jokes and English humorists, as he appreciated at a deeper level a uniquely native masterpiece like *Wuthering Heights*. He really liked the British, had visited this country several times, envied us our political institutions, and greatly honoured the genius of our religious poets and mystics. It was on his last visit a few years before the war that he prefaced a lecture on Mysticism by remarking that for a foreigner to come to tell an English audience about Mysticism was 'to bring owls to Athens' (or as we should say, coals to Newcastle). Certainly no one who saw his erect soldierly figure with the Kaiser moustache would have guessed that he was a scholar who hated militarism, and whose death after many years of poor health was hastened by the heartbreaking experience of the first years of Hitler's pagan *Reich*.

For widely as his mind ranged among the world's religions it must be emphasized that this scholar and thinker was no dilettante culling inspiring ideas and glimpses at second hand, as a man might make an anthology of fine passages from poets or sages. He was himself rooted in the Christian faith, a committed man, to whom the central truth in religion was the worship of God as revealed in Christ.

FOREWORD BY THE AUTHOR

IN this book I have ventured to write of that which may be called 'non-rational' or 'supra-rational' in the depths of the divine nature. I do not thereby want to promote in any way the tendency of our time towards an extravagant and fantastic 'irrationalism', but rather to join issue with it in its morbid form. The 'irrational' is to-day a favourite theme of all who are too lazy to think or too ready to evade the arduous duty of clarifying their ideas and grounding their convictions on a basis of coherent thought. This book, recognizing the profound import of the non-rational for metaphysic, makes a serious attempt to analyse all the more exactly the *feeling* which remains where the *concept* fails, and to introduce a terminology which is not any the more loose or indeterminate for having necessarily to make use of *symbols*.

Before I ventured upon this field of inquiry I spent many years of study upon the *rational* aspect of that supreme Reality we call 'God', and the results of my work are contained in my books, *Naturalistische und religiöse Weltansicht* (Eng. tr. *Naturalism and Religion*. London, 1907), and *Die Kant-Friesische Religions-Philosophie*. And I feel that no one ought to concern himself with the *Numen ineffabile* who has not already devoted assiduous and serious study to the *Ratio aeterna*.

This foreword gives me a very welcome opportunity to express my thanks to the translator for his care, his remarkable delicacy of interpretation, and for the valuable supplementary pages he has added. An English critic has said that 'the translation is much better than the original'; and to this I have nothing to object.

RUDOLF OTTO

MARBURG
1923

Das Schaudern ist der Menschheit bestes Teil.
Wie auch die Welt ihm das Gefühl verteuere,
Ergriffen fühlt er tief das Ungeheuere.

CHAPTER I

The Rational and the Non-Rational

IT is essential to every theistic conception of God, and most of all to the Christian, that it designates and precisely characterizes deity by the attributes spirit, reason, purpose, good will, supreme power, unity, selfhood. The nature of God is thus thought of by analogy with our human nature of reason and personality; only, whereas in ourselves we are aware of this as qualified by restriction and limitation, as applied to God the attributes we use are 'completed', i.e. thought as absolute and unqualified. Now all these attributes constitute clear and definite *concepts*: they can be grasped by the intellect; they can be analysed by thought; they even admit of definition. An object that can thus be thought conceptually may be termed *rational*. The nature of deity described in the attributes above mentioned is, then, a rational nature; and a religion which recognizes and maintains such a view of God is in so far a 'rational' religion. Only on such terms is *belief* possible in contrast to mere *feeling*. And Christianity at least it is false that 'feeling is all, the na. but sound and smoke';[1] – where 'name' stands for conception or thought. Rather we count this the very mark and criterion of a religion's high rank and superior value: that it should have no lack of *conceptions* about God; that it should admit knowledge – the knowledge that comes by faith – of the transcendent in terms of conceptual thought, whether those already mentioned or others which continue and develop them. Christianity not only possesses such conceptions but possesses them in unique clarity and abundance, and this is, though not the sole or even the chief, yet a very real sign of its superiority over religions of other forms and at other levels. This must be asserted at the outset and with the most positive emphasis.

1. Goethe, *Faust*.

But, when this is granted, we have to be on our guard against an error which would lead to a wrong and one-sided interpretation of religion. This is the view that the essence of deity can be given completely and exhaustively in such 'rational' attributions as have been referred to above and in others like them. It is not an unnatural misconception. We are prompted to it by the traditional language of edification, with its characteristic phraseology and ideas; by the learned treatment of religious themes in sermon and theological instruction; and further even by our Holy Scriptures themselves. In all these cases the 'rational' element occupies the foreground, and often nothing else seems to be present at all. But this is after all to be expected. All language, in so far as it consists of words, purports to convey ideas or concepts – that is what language means – and the more clearly and unequivocally it does so, the better the language. And hence expositions of religious truth in language inevitably tend to stress the 'rational' attributes of God.

But though the above mistake is thus a natural one enough, it is none the less seriously misleading. For so far are these 'rational' attributes from exhausting the idea of deity, that they in fact imply a non-rational or supra-rational Subject of which they are predicates. They are 'essential' (and not merely 'accidental') attributes of that subject, but they are also, it is important to notice, *synthetic* essential attributes. That is to say, we have to predicate them of a subject which they qualify, but which in its deeper essence is not, nor indeed can be, comprehended in them; which rather requires comprehension of a quite different kind. Yet, though it eludes the conceptual way of understanding, it must be in some way or other within our grasp, else absolutely nothing could be asserted of it. And even mysticism, in speaking of it as τὸ ἄρρητον, the ineffable, does not really mean to imply that absolutely nothing can be asserted of the object of the religious consciousness; otherwise, mysticism could exist only in unbroken silence, whereas what has generally been a characteristic of the mystics is their copious eloquence.

Here for the first time we come up against the contrast

between rationalism and profounder religion, and with this contrast and its signs we shall be repeatedly concerned in what follows. We have here in fact the first and most distinctive mark of rationalism, with which all the rest are bound up. It is not that which is commonly asserted, that rationalism is the denial, and its opposite the affirmation, of the miraculous. That is manifestly a wrong or at least a very superficial distinction. For the traditional theory of the miraculous as the occasional breach in the causal nexus in nature by a Being who himself instituted and must therefore be master of it – this theory is itself as massively 'rational' as it is possible to be. Rationalists have often enough acquiesced in the possibility of the miraculous in this sense; they have even themselves contributed to frame a theory of it: whereas anti-rationalists have been often indifferent to the whole controversy about miracles. The difference between rationalism and its opposite is to be found elsewhere. It resolves itself rather into a peculiar difference of *quality* in the mental attitude and emotional content of the religious life itself. All depends upon this: in our idea of God is the non-rational overborne, even perhaps wholly excluded, by the rational? Or conversely, does the non-rational itself preponderate over the rational? Looking at the matter thus, we see that the common dictum, that orthodoxy itself has been the mother of rationalism, is in some measure well founded. It is not simply that orthodoxy was preoccupied with doctrine and the framing of dogma, for these have been no less a concern of the wildest mystics. It is rather that orthodoxy found in the construction of dogma and doctrine no way to do justice to the non-rational aspect of its subject. So far from keeping the non-rational element in religion alive in the heart of the religious experience, orthodox Christianity manifestly failed to recognize its value, and by this failure gave to the idea of God a one-sidedly intellectualistic and rationalistic interpretation.

This bias to rationalization still prevails, not only in theology but in the science of comparative religion in general, and from top to bottom of it. The modern students of mythology, and those who pursue research into the religion of 'primitive man' and attempt to reconstruct the 'bases' or 'sources' of religion, are all victims to it. Men do not, of course, in these cases employ those lofty 'rational' concepts which we took as our point of departure; but they tend to take these concepts and their gradual 'evolution' as setting the main problem of their inquiry, and fashion ideas and notions of lower value, which they regard as paving the way for them. It is always in terms of concepts and ideas that the subject is pursued, 'natural' ones, moreover, such as have a place in the general sphere of man's ideational life, and are not specifically 'religious'. And then with a resolution and cunning which one can hardly help admiring, men shut their eyes to that which is quite unique in the religious experience, even in its most primitive manifestations. But it is rather a matter for astonishment than for admiration! For if there be any single domain of human experience that presents us with something unmistakably specific and unique, peculiar to itself, assuredly it is that of the religious life. In truth the enemy has often a keener vision in this matter than either the champion of religion or the neutral and professedly impartial theorist. For the adversaries on their side know very well that the entire 'pother about mysticism' has nothing to do with 'reason' and 'rationality'.

And so it is salutary that we should be incited to notice that religion is not exclusively contained and exhaustively comprised in any series of 'rational' assertions; and it is well worth while to attempt to bring the relation of the different 'moments' of religion to one another clearly before the mind, so that its nature may become more manifest.

This attempt we are now to make with respect to the quite distinctive category of the holy or sacred.

CHAPTER II

'Numen' and the 'Numinous'

'HOLINESS' – 'the holy' – is a category of interpretation and valuation peculiar to the sphere of religion. It is, indeed, applied by transference to another sphere – that of ethics – but it is not itself derived from this. While it is complex, it contains a quite specific element or 'moment', which sets it apart from 'the rational' in the meaning we gave to that word above, and which remains inexpressible – an ἄρρητον or *ineffabile* – in the sense that it completely eludes apprehension in terms of concepts. The same thing is true (to take a quite different region of experience) of the category of the beautiful.

Now these statements would be untrue from the outset if 'the holy' were merely what is meant by the word, not only in common parlance, but in philosophical, and generally even in theological usage. The fact is we have come to use the words 'holy', 'sacred' (*heilig*) in an entirely derivative sense, quite different from that which they originally bore. We generally take 'holy' as meaning 'completely good'; it is the absolute moral attribute, denoting the consummation of moral goodness. In this sense Kant calls the will which remains unwaveringly obedient to the moral law from the motive of duty a 'holy' will; here clearly we have simply the *perfectly moral* will. In the same way we may speak of the holiness or sanctity of duty or law, meaning merely that they are imperative upon conduct and universally obligatory.

But this common usage of the term is inaccurate. It is true that all this moral significance is contained in the word 'holy', but it includes in addition – as even we cannot but feel – a clear overplus of meaning, and this it is now our task to isolate. Nor is this merely a later or acquired meaning; rather 'holy', or at least the equivalent words in Latin and Greek, in Semitic and other ancient languages, denoted first and foremost *only* this overplus: if the ethical element was present at all, at any rate it was not original and never constituted the whole meaning of the word. Anyone who uses it to-day does undoubtedly always feel 'the morally good' to be implied in 'holy'; and accordingly in our inquiry into that element which is separate and peculiar to the idea of the holy it will be useful, at least for the temporary purpose of the investigation, to invent a special term to stand for 'the holy' *minus* its moral factor or 'moment', and, as we can now add, minus its 'rational' aspect altogether.

It will be our endeavour to suggest this unnamed Something to the reader as far as we may, so that he may himself feel it. There is no religion in which it does not live as the real innermost core, and without it no religion would be worthy of the name. It is pre-eminently a living force in the Semitic religions, and of these again in none has it such vigour as in that of the Bible. Here, too, it has a name of its own, viz. the Hebrew *qādôsh*, to which the Greek ἅγιος and the Latin *sanctus*, and, more accurately still, *sacer*, are the corresponding terms. It is not, of course, disputed that these terms in all three languages connote, as part of their meaning, *good*, *absolute goodness*, when, that is, the notion has ripened and reached the highest stage in its development. And we then use the word 'holy' to translate them. But this 'holy' then represents the gradual shaping and filling in with ethical meaning, or what we shall call the 'schematization', of what was a unique original feeling-response, which can be in itself ethically neutral and claims consideration in its own right. And when this moment or element first emerges and begins its long development, all those expressions (*qādôsh*, ἅγιος, *sacer*, etc.) mean beyond all question something quite other than 'the good'. This is universally agreed by contemporary criticism, which rightly explains the rendering of *qādôsh* by 'good' as a mistranslation and unwarranted 'rationalization' or 'moralization' of the term.

Accordingly, it is worth while, as we have said, to find a word to stand for this element in isolation, this 'extra' in the meaning of 'holy' above and beyond the meaning of goodness. By means of a special term we shall the better be able, first, to keep the meaning clearly apart and distinct, and second, to apprehend and classify connectedly whatever subordinate forms or stages of development it may show. For this purpose I adopt a word coined from the Latin *numen*. *Omen* has given us 'ominous', and there is no reason why from *numen* we should not similarly form a word 'numinous'. I shall speak, then of a unique 'numinous' category of value and of a definitely 'numinous' state of mind, which is always found wherever the category is applied. This mental state is perfectly *sui generis* and irreducible to any other; and therefore, like every absolutely primary and elementary datum, while it admits of being discussed, it cannot be strictly defined. There is only one way to help another to an understanding of it. He must be guided and led on by consideration and discussion of the matter through the ways of his own mind, until he reach the point at which 'the numinous' in him perforce begins to stir, to start into life and into consciousness. We can cooperate in this process by bringing before his notice all that can be found in other regions of the mind, already known and familiar, to resemble, or again to afford some special contrast to, the particular experience we wish to elucidate. Then we must add: 'This *X* of ours is not precisely *this* experience, but akin to this one and the opposite of that other. Cannot you now realize for yourself what it is?' In other words our *X* cannot, strictly speaking, be taught, it can only be evoked, awakened in the mind; as everything that comes 'of the spirit' must be awakened.

CHAPTER III

The Elements in the 'Numinous'

CREATURE-FEELING

THE reader is invited to direct his mind to a moment of deeply-felt religious experience, as little as possible qualified by other forms of consciousness. Whoever cannot do this, whoever knows no such moments in his experience, is requested to read no further; for it is not easy to discuss questions of religious psychology with one who can recollect the emotions of his adolescence, the discomforts of indigestion, or say, social feelings, but cannot recall any intrinsically religious feelings. We do not blame such an one, when he tries for himself to advance as far as he can with the help of such principles of explanation as he knows, interpreting 'aesthetics' in terms of sensuous pleasure, and 'religion' as a function of the gregarious instinct and social standards, or as something more primitive still. But the artist, who for his part has an intimate personal knowledge of the distinctive element in the aesthetic experience, will decline his theories with thanks, and the religious man will reject them even more uncompromisingly.

Next, in the probing and analysis of such states of the soul as that of solemn worship, it will be well if regard be paid to what is unique in them rather than to what they have in common with other similar states. To be *rapt* in worship is one thing; to be morally *uplifted* by the contemplation of a good deed is another; and it is not to their common features, but to those elements of emotional content peculiar to the first that we would have attention directed as precisely as possible. As Christians we undoubtedly here first meet with feelings familiar enough in a weaker form in other departments of experience, such as feelings of gratitude, trust, love, reliance, humble submission, and dedication. But this does not by any means exhaust the content of religious worship. Not in any of these have we got the special features of the quite unique and incomparable experience of solemn worship. In what does this consist?

Schleiermacher has the credit of isolating a very important element in such an experience. This is the 'feeling of dependence'. But this important discovery of Schleiermacher is open to criticism in more than one respect.

In the first place, the feeling or emotion which he really has in mind in this phrase is in its specific quality not a 'feeling of dependence' in the 'natural' sense of the word. As such, other domains of life and other regions of experience than the religious occasion the feeling, as a sense of personal insufficiency and impotence, a consciousness of being determined by circumstances and environment. The feeling of which Schleiermacher wrote has an undeniable analogy with these states of mind: they serve as an indication to it, and its nature may be elucidated by them, so that, by following the direction in which they point, the feeling itself may be spontaneously felt. But the feeling is at the same time also qualitatively different from such analogous states of mind. Schleiermacher himself, in a way, recognizes this by distinguishing the feeling of pious or religious dependence from all other feelings of dependence. His mistake is in making the distinction merely that between 'absolute' and 'relative' dependence, and therefore a difference of degree and not of intrinsic quality. What he overlooks is that, in giving the feeling the name 'feeling of dependence' at all, we are really employing what is no more than a very close analogy. Anyone who compares and contrasts the two states of mind introspectively will find out, I think, what I mean. It cannot be expressed by means of anything else, just because it is so primary and elementary a datum in our psychical life, and therefore only definable through itself. It may perhaps help him if I cite a well-known example, in which the precise 'moment' or element of religious feeling of which we are speaking is most actively present. When Abraham ventures to plead with God for the men of Sodom, he says (Gen. xviii.

27): 'Behold now, I have taken upon me to speak unto the Lord, which am but dust and ashes.' There you have a self-confessed 'feeling of dependence', which is yet at the same time far more than, and something other than, *merely* a feeling of dependence. Desiring to give it a name of its own, I propose to call it 'creature-consciousness' or creature-feeling. It is the emotion of a creature, submerged and overwhelmed by its own nothingness in contrast to that which is supreme above all creatures.

It is easily seen that, once again, this phrase, whatever it is, is not a *conceptual* explanation of the matter. All that this new term 'creature-feeling' can express, is the note of submergence into nothingness before an overpowering, absolute might of some kind; whereas everything turns upon the *character* of this overpowering might, a character which cannot be expressed verbally, and can only be suggested indirectly through the tone and content of a man's feeling-response to it. And this response must be directly experienced in oneself to be understood.

We have now to note a second defect in the formulation of Schleiermacher's principle. The religious category discovered by him, by whose means he professes to determine the real content of the religious emotion, is merely a category of *self*-valuation, in the sense of self-depreciation. According to him the religious emotion would be directly and primarily a sort of *self*-consciousness, a feeling concerning oneself in a special determined relation, viz. one's dependence. Thus, according to Schleiermacher, I can only come upon the very fact of God as the result of an inference, that is, by reasoning to a cause beyond myself to account for my 'feeling of dependence'. But this is entirely opposed to the psychological facts of the case. Rather, the 'creature-feeling' is itself a first subjective concomitant and effect of another feeling-element, which casts it like a shadow, but which in itself indubitably has immediate and primary reference to an object outside the self.[1]

1. This is so manifestly borne out by experience that it must be about the first thing to force itself upon the notice of psychologists analysing the facts of religion. There is a certain naïveté in the

Now this object is just what we have already spoken of as 'the numinous'. For the 'creature-feeling' and the sense of dependence to arise in the mind the 'numen' must be experienced as present, a *numen praesens*, as is in the case of Abraham. There must be felt a something 'numinous', something bearing the character of a 'numen', to which the mind turns spontaneously; or (which is the same thing in other words) these feelings can only arise in the mind as accompanying emotions when the category of 'the numinous' is called into play.

The numinous is thus felt as objective and outside the self. We have now to inquire more closely into its nature and the modes of its manifestations.

following passage from William James's *Varieties of Religious Experience* (p. 58), where, alluding to the origin of the Grecian representations of the gods, he says: 'As regards the origin of the Greek gods, we need not at present seek an opinion. But the whole array of our instances leads to a conclusion something like this: It is as if there were in the human consciousness a *sense of reality*, *a feeling of objective presence*, a *perception* of what we may call *"something there"*, more deep and more general than any of the special and particular "senses" by which the current psychology supposes existent realities to be originally revealed.' (The italics are James's own.) James is debarred by his empiricist and pragmatist standpoint from coming to a recognition of faculties of knowledge and potentialities of thought in the spirit itself, and he is therefore obliged to have recourse to somewhat singular and mysterious hypotheses to explain this fact. But he grasps the fact itself clearly enough and is sufficient of a realist not to explain it away. But this 'feeling of reality', the feeling of a 'numinous' *object* objectively given, must be posited as a primary immediate datum of consciousness, and the 'feeling of dependence' is then a consequence, following very closely upon it, viz. a depreciation of the *subject* in his own eyes. The latter presupposes the former.

'Mysterium Tremendum'

THE ANALYSIS OF 'TREMENDUM'

WE said above that the nature of the numinous can only be suggested by means of the special way in which it is reflected in the mind in terms of feeling. 'Its nature is such that it grips or stirs the human mind with this and that determinate affective state.' We have now to attempt to give a further indication of these determinate states. We must once again endeavour, by adducing feelings akin to them for the purpose of analogy or contrast, and by the use of metaphor and symbolic expressions, to make the states of mind we are investigating ring out, as it were, of themselves.

Let us consider the deepest and most fundamental element in all strong and sincerely felt religious emotion. Faith unto salvation, trust, love – all these are there. But over and above these is an element which may also on occasion, quite apart from them, profoundly affect us and occupy the mind with a wellnigh bewildering strength. Let us follow it up with every effort of sympathy and imaginative intuition wherever it is to be found, in the lives of those around us, in sudden, strong ebullitions of personal piety and the frames of mind such ebullitions evince, in the fixed and ordered solemnities of rites and liturgies, and again in the atmosphere that clings to old religious monuments and buildings, to temples and to churches. If we do so we shall find we are dealing with something for which there is only one appropriate expression, '*mysterium tremendum*'. The feeling of it may at times come sweeping like a gentle tide, pervading the mind with a tranquil mood of deepest worship. It may pass over into a more set and lasting attitude of the soul, continuing, as it were, thrillingly vibrant and resonant, until at last it dies away and the soul resumes its 'profane', non-religious mood of everyday experience. It may burst in sudden eruption up from the depths of the soul with spasms and convulsions, or lead to the strangest excitements, to intoxicated frenzy, to transport, and to ecstasy. It has its wild and demonic forms and can sink to an almost grisly horror and shuddering. It has its crude, barbaric antecedents and early manifestations, and again it may be developed into something beautiful and pure and glorious. It may become the hushed, trembling, and speechless humility of the creature in the presence of – whom or what? In the presence of that which is a *mystery* inexpressible and above all creatures.

It is again evident at once that here too our attempted formulation by means of a concept is once more a merely negative one. Conceptually *mysterium* denotes merely that which is hidden and esoteric, that which is beyond conception or understanding, extraordinary and unfamiliar. The term does not define the object more positively in its qualitative character. But though what is enunciated in the word is negative, what is meant is something absolutely and intensely positive. This pure positive we can experience in feelings – feelings which our discussion can help to make clear to us, in so far as it arouses them actually in our hearts.

The Element of Awefulness

To get light upon the positive '*quale*' of the object of these feelings, we must analyse more closely our phrase *mysterium tremendum*, and we will begin first with the adjective.

Tremor is in itself merely the perfectly familiar and 'natural' emotion of *fear*. But here the term is taken, aptly enough but still only by analogy, to denote a quite specific kind of emotional response, wholly distinct from that of being afraid, though it so far resembles it that the analogy of fear may be used to throw light upon its nature. There are in some languages special expressions which denote, either exclusively or in the first instance, this 'fear' that is more than fear proper. The Hebrew *hiqdīsh* (hallow) is an example. To 'keep a thing holy in the heart' means to mark it off by a feeling of peculiar dread, not to be mistaken for any ordinary dread, that is, to appraise it by the category of the numinous. But the Old Testament throughout is rich in parallel expressions for this feeling. Specially noticeable is the *'ēmāh* of Yahweh ('fear of God'), which Yahweh can pour forth, dispatching almost like a daemon, and which seizes upon a man with paralysing effect. It is closely related to the δεῖμα πανικόν of the Greeks. Compare Exod. xxiii. 27: 'I will send my fear before thee, and will destroy all the people to whom thou shalt come . . .'; also Job ix. 34; xiii. 21 ('let not his fear terrify me'; 'let not thy dread make me afraid'). Here we have a terror fraught with an inward shuddering such as not even the most menacing and overpowering created thing can instil. It has something spectral in it.

In the Greek language we have a corresponding term in σεβαστός. The early Christians could clearly feel that the title Σεβαστός (*Augustus*) was one that could not fittingly be given to any creature, not even to the emperor. They felt that to call a man σεβαστός was to give a human being a name proper only to the *numen*, to rank him by the category proper only to the *numen*, and that it therefore amounted to a kind of idolatry. Of modern languages English has the words 'awe', 'aweful', which in their deeper and most special sense approximate closely to our meaning. The phrase, 'he stood aghast', is also suggestive in this connexion. On the other hand, German has no native-grown expression of its own for the higher and riper form of the emotion we are considering, unless it be in a word like *erschauern*, which does suggest it fairly well. It is far otherwise with its cruder and more debased phases, where such terms as *grausen* and *Schauer*, and the more popular and telling *gruseln* ('grue'), *gräsen*, and *grässlich* ('grisly'), very clearly designate the numinous element. In my examination of Wundt's Animism I suggested the term *Scheu* (dread); but the special 'numinous' quality (making it 'awe' rather than 'dread' in the ordinary sense) would then, of course, have to be denoted by inverted commas. 'Religious dread' (or 'awe') would perhaps be a better designation. Its antecedent stage is 'daemonic dread' (cf. the horror of Pan) with its queer perversion, a sort of abortive offshoot, the 'dread of ghosts'. It first begins to stir in the feeling of 'something uncanny', 'eerie', or 'weird'. It is this feeling which, emerging in the mind of primeval man, forms the starting-point for the entire religious development in history. 'Daemons' and 'gods' alike spring from this root, and all the products of 'mythological apperception' or 'fantasy' are nothing but different modes in which it has been objectified. And all ostensible explanations of the origin of religion in terms of animism or magic or folk-psychology are doomed from the outset to wander astray and miss the real goal of their inquiry, unless they recognize this fact of our nature – primary, unique, underivable from anything else – to be the basic factor and the basic impulse underlying the entire process of religious evolution.[1]

Not only is the saying of Luther, that the natural man cannot fear God, perfectly correct from the standpoint of psychology, but we ought to go farther and add that the natural man is quite unable even to 'shudder' (*grauen*) or feel horror in the real sense of the word. For 'shuddering' is something more than 'natural', ordinary fear. It implies that the mysterious is already beginning to loom before the mind, to touch the feelings. It implies the first application of a category of valuation which has no place in the everyday natural world of ordinary experience, and is only possible to a being in whom has been awakened a mental predisposition, unique in kind and different in a definite way from any 'natural' faculty. And this

1. Cf. my papers in *Theologische Rundschau*, 1910, vol. i, on 'Myth and Religion in Wundt's *Völkerpsychologie*', and in *Deutsche Literaturzeitung*, 1910, No. 38. I find in more recent investigations, especially those of R. R. Marett and N. Söderblom, a very welcome confirmation of the positions I there maintained. It is true that neither of them calls attention quite as precisely as, in this matter, psychologists need to do, to the unique character of the religious 'awe' and its qualitative distinction from all 'natural' feelings. But Marett more particularly comes within a hair's breadth of what I take to be the truth about the matter. Cf. his *Threshold of Religion*, London, 1909, and N. Söderblom's *Das Werden des Gottesglaubens*, Leipzig, 1915, also my review of the latter in *Theol. Literaturzeitung* (January 1915).

newly-revealed capacity, even in the crude and violent manifest-ations which are all it at first evinces, bears witness to a com-pletely new function of experience and standard of valuation, only belonging to the spirit of man.

Before going on to consider the elements which unfold as the '*tremendum*' develops, let us give a little further consideration to the first crude, primitive forms in which this 'numinous dread' or *awe* shows itself. It is the mark which really charac-terizes the so-called 'religion of primitive man', and there it appears as 'daemonic dread'. This crudely naïve and pri-mordial emotional disturbance, and the fantastic images to which it gives rise, are later overborne and ousted by more highly developed forms of the numinous emotion, with all its mysteriously impelling power. But even when this has long attained its higher and purer mode of expression it is possible for the primitive types of excitation that were formerly a part of it to break out in the soul in all their original naïveté and so to be experienced afresh. That this is so is shown by the potent attraction again and again exercised by the element of horror and 'shudder' in ghost stories, even among persons of high all-round education. It is a remarkable fact that the physical reaction to which this unique 'dread' of the uncanny gives rise is also unique, and is not found in the case of any 'natural' fear or terror. We say: 'my blood ran icy cold', and 'my flesh crept'. The 'cold blood' feeling may be a symptom of ordinary, natural fear, but there is something non-natural or supernatural about the symptom of 'creeping flesh'. And anyone who is capable of more precise intro-spection must recognize that the distinction between such a 'dread' and natural fear is not simply one of degree and intensity. The awe or 'dread' *may* indeed be so overwhelm-ingly great that it seems to penetrate to the very marrow, making the man's hair bristle and his limbs quake. But it may also steal upon him almost unobserved as the gentlest of agitations, a mere fleeting shadow passing across his mood. It has therefore nothing to do with intensity, and no natural fear passes over into it merely by being intensified. I may be beyond all measure afraid and terrified without there being even a trace of the feeling of uncanniness in my emotion.

We should see the facts more clearly if psychology in general would make a more decisive endeavour to examine and classify the feelings and emotions according to their qualitative differences. But the far too rough division of elementary feelings in general into pleasures and pains is still an obstacle to this. In point of fact 'pleasures' no more than other feelings are differentiated merely by degrees of intensity: they show very definite and specific differences. It makes a specific difference to the condition of mind whether the soul is merely in a state of pleasure, or joy, or aesthetic rapture, or moral exaltation, or finally in the religious bliss that may come in worship. Such states certainly show resemblances one to another, and on that account can legitimately be brought under a common class-concept ('pleasure'), which serves to cut them off from other psychical functions, generically different. But this class-concept, so far from turning the various subordinate species into merely different degrees of the same thing, can do nothing at all to throw light upon the essence of each several state of mind which it includes.

Though the numinous emotion in its completest development shows a world of difference from the mere 'daemonic dread', yet not even at the highest level does it belie its pedigree or kindred. Even when the worship of 'daemons' has long since reached the higher level of worship of 'gods', these gods still retain as *numina* something of the 'ghost' in the impress they make on the feelings of the worshipper, viz. the peculiar quality of the 'uncanny' and 'aweful', which survives with the quality of exaltedness and sublimity or is symbolized by means of it. And this element, softened though it is, does not disappear even on the highest level of all, where the worship of God is at its purest. Its disappearance would be indeed an essential loss. The 'shudder' reappears in a form ennobled beyond measure where the soul, held speechless, trembles inwardly to the farthest fibre of its being. It invades the mind mightily in Christian worship with the words: 'Holy, holy, holy'; it breaks forth from the hymn of Tersteegen:

God Himself is present:
Heart, be stilled before Him:
Prostrate, inwardly adore Him.

The 'shudder' has here lost its crazy and bewildering note, but not the ineffable something that holds the mind. It has become a mystical awe, and sets free as its accompaniment, reflected in self-consciousness, that 'creature-feeling' that has already been described as the feeling of personal nothingness and submergence before the awe-inspiring object directly experienced.

The referring of this feeling of numinous *tremor* to its object in the numen brings into relief a property of the latter which plays an important part in our Holy Scriptures, and which has been the occasion of many difficulties, both to commentators and to theologians, from its puzzling and baffling nature. This is the ὀργή (*orgé*), the Wrath of Yahweh, which recurs in the New Testament as ὀργὴ θεοῦ, and which is clearly analogous to the idea occurring in many religions of a mysterious *ira deorum*. To pass through the Indian Pantheon of gods is to find deities who seem to be made up altogether out of such an ὀργή; and even the higher Indian gods of grace and pardon have frequently, beside their merciful, their 'wrath' form. But as regards the 'wrath of Yahweh', the strange features about it have for long been a matter for constant remark. In the first place, it is patent from many passages of the Old Testament that this 'wrath' has no concern whatever with moral qualities. There is something very baffling in the way in which it 'is kindled' and manifested. It is, as has been well said, 'like a hidden force of nature', like stored-up electricity, discharging itself upon anyone who comes too near. It is 'incalculable' and 'arbitrary'. Anyone who is accustomed to think of deity only by its rational attributes must see in this 'wrath' mere caprice and wilful passion. But such a view would have been emphatically rejected by the religious men of the Old Covenant, for to them the Wrath of God, so far from being a diminution of His Godhead, appears as a natural expression of it, an element of 'holiness' itself, and a quite indispensable

entirely right. This ὀργή is nothing
pprehended and expressed by the
om the domain of natural experience,
rdinary passional life of men. But naïve
analogy is most disconcertingly apt and
h so that it will always retain its value and
ss than for the men of old be an inevitable way
sing one element in the religious emotion. It can-
doubted that, despite the protest of Schleiermacher and
hl, Christianity also has something to teach of the 'wrath
God'.

It will be again at once apparent that in the use of this word we are not concerned with a genuine intellectual 'concept', but only with a sort of illustrative substitute for a concept. 'Wrath' here is the 'ideogram' of a unique emotional moment in religious experience, a moment whose singularly *daunting* and awe-inspiring character must be gravely disturbing to those persons who will recognize nothing in the divine nature but goodness, gentleness, love, and a sort of confidential intimacy— in a word, only those aspects of God which turn towards the world of men.

This ὀργή is thus quite wrongly spoken of as 'natural' wrath: rather it is an entirely non- or super-natural, i.e. numinous, quality. The rationalization process takes place when it begins to be filled in with elements derived from the moral reason: righteousness in requital, and punishment for moral transgression. But it should be noted that the idea of the wrath of God in the Bible is always a synthesis, in which the original is combined with the later meaning that has come to fill it in. Something supra-rational throbs and gleams, palpable and visible, in the 'wrath of God', prompting to a sense of 'terror' that no 'natural' anger can arouse.

Beside the 'wrath' or 'anger' of Yahweh stands the related expression 'jealousy of Yahweh'. The state of mind denoted by the phrase 'being jealous *for* Yahweh' is also a numinous state of mind, in which features of the *tremendum* pass over into the man who has experience of it.

The Element of 'Overpoweringness' ('majestas')

We have been attempting to unfold the implications
aspect of the *mysterium tremendum* indicated by the adj
and the result so far may be summarized in two words,
stituting, as before, what may be called an 'ideogram', ra
than a concept proper, viz. 'absolute unapproachability'.

It will be felt at once that there is yet a further elemen
which must be added, that, namely, of 'might', 'power', 'absolute overpoweringness'. We will take to represent this the term
majestas, majesty – the more readily because anyone with a
feeling for language must detect a last faint trace of the
numinous still clinging to the word. The *tremendum* may then
be rendered more adequately *tremenda majestas*, or 'aweful
majesty'. This second element of majesty may continue to be
vividly preserved, where the first, that of unapproachability,
recedes and dies away, as may be seen, for example, in mysticism. It is especially in relation to this element of majesty or
absolute overpoweringness that the creature-consciousness, of
which we have already spoken, comes upon the scene, as a sort
of shadow or subjective reflection of it. Thus, in contrast to
'the overpowering' of which we are conscious as an object over
against the self, there is the feeling of one's own submergence,
of being but 'dust and ashes' and nothingness. And this forms
the numinous raw material for the feeling of religious humility.[1]

Here we must revert once again to Schleiermacher's expression for what we call 'creature-feeling', viz. the 'feeling of
dependence'. We found fault with this phrase before on the
ground that Schleiermacher thereby takes as basis and point
of departure what is merely a secondary effect; that he sets out
to teach a consciousness of the religious *object* only by way of
an inference from the shadow it casts upon *self*-consciousness.
We have now a further criticism to bring against it, and it is
this. By 'feeling of dependence' Schleiermacher means consciousness of *being conditioned* (as effect by cause), and so he
develops the implications of this logically enough in his sections

1. Cf. R. R. Marett. 'The Birth of Humility', in *The Threshold of
Religion*, 2nd ed., 1914. [Tr.]

upon Creation and Preservation. On the side of the deity the correlate to 'dependence' would thus be 'causality', i.e. God's character as all-causing and all-conditioning. But a sense of this does not enter at all into that immediate and first-hand religious emotion which we have in the moment of worship, and which we can recover in a measure for analysis; it belongs on the contrary decidedly to the *rational* side of the idea of God; its implications admit of precise conceptual determination; and it springs from quite a distinct source. The difference between the 'feeling of dependence' of Schleiermacher and that which finds typical utterance in the words of Abraham already cited might be expressed as that between the consciousness of *createdness*[1] and the consciousness of *creaturehood*.[2] In the one case you have the creature as the work of the divine creative act; in the other, impotence and general nothingness as against over-powering might, dust and ashes as against 'majesty'. In the one case you have the fact of having been created; in the other, the status of the creature. And as soon as speculative thought has come to concern itself with this latter type of consciousness – as soon as it has come to analyse this 'majesty' – we are introduced to a set of ideas quite different from those of creation or preservation. We come upon the ideas, first, of the annihilation of self, and then, as its complement, of the transcendent as the sole and entire reality. These are the characteristic notes of mysticism in all its forms, however otherwise various in content. For one of the chiefest and most general features of mysticism is just this *self-depreciation* (so plainly parallel to the case of Abraham), the estimation of the self, of the personal 'I', as something not perfectly or essentially real, or even as mere nullity, a self-depreciation which comes to demand its own fulfilment in practice in rejecting the delusion of selfhood, and so makes for the annihilation of the self. And on the other hand mysticism leads to a valuation of the transcendent object of its reference as that which through plenitude of being stands supreme and absolute, so that the finite self contrasted with it becomes conscious even in its nullity that 'I am naught, Thou

1. *Geschaffenheit.*
2. *Geschöpflichkeit.*

art all'. There is no thought in this of any causal relation between God, the creator, and the self, the creature. The point from which speculation starts is not a 'consciousness of absolute dependence' – of myself as result and effect of a divine cause – for that would in point of fact lead to insistence upon the reality of the self; it starts from a consciousness of the absolute superiority or supremacy of a power other than myself, and it is only as it falls back upon ontological terms to achieve its end – terms generally borrowed from natural science – that that element of the *tremendum*, originally apprehended as 'plenitude of power', becomes transmuted into 'plenitude of being'.

This leads again to the mention of mysticism. No mere inquiry into the genesis of a thing can throw any light upon its essential nature, and it is hence immaterial to us how mysticism historically arose. But essentially mysticism is the stressing to a very high degree, indeed the overstressing, of the non-rational or supra-rational elements in religion; and it is only intelligible when so understood. The various phases and factors of the non-rational may receive varying emphasis, and the type of mysticism will differ according as some or others fall into the background. What we have been analysing, however, is a feature that recurs in all forms of mysticism everywhere, and it is nothing but the 'creature-consciousness' stressed to the utmost and to excess, the expression meaning, if we may repeat the contrast already made, not 'feeling of our createdness' but 'feeling of our creaturehood', that is the consciousness of the littleness of every creature in face of that which is above all creatures.

A characteristic common to all types of mysticism is the *Identification*, in different degrees of completeness, of the personal self with the transcendent Reality. This identification has a source of its own, with which we are not here concerned, and springs from 'moments' of religious experience which would require separate treatment. 'Identification' alone, however, is not enough for mysticism; it must be Identification with the Something that is at once absolutely supreme in power and reality and wholly non-rational. And it is among the mystics that we most encounter this element of religious consciousness. Récéjac has noticed this in his *Essai sur les fondements de la connaissance mystique*. Paris, 1897. He writes (p. 90):

Le mysticisme commence par la crainte, par le sentiment d'une *domination* universelle, *invincible*, et devient plus tard un désir d'union avec ce qui domine ainsi.

And some very clear examples of this taken from the religious experience of the present day are to be found in W. James (op. cit., p. 66):

The perfect stillness of the night was thrilled by a more solemn silence. The darkness held a presence that was all the more felt because it was not seen. I could not any more have doubted that *He* was there than that I was. Indeed, I felt myself to be, if possible, the less real of the two.

This example is particularly instructive as to the relation of mysticism to the 'feelings of identification', for the experience here recounted was on the point of passing into it.[1]

The Element of 'Energy' or Urgency

There is, finally, a third element comprised in those of *tremendum* and *majestas*, awefulness and majesty, and this I venture to call the 'urgency' or 'energy' of the numinous object. It is particularly vividly perceptible in the ὀργή or 'wrath'; and it everywhere clothes itself in symbolical expressions – vitality, passion, emotional temper, will, force, movement,[2] excitement, activity, impetus. These features are typical and recur again and again from the daemonic level up to the idea of the 'living' God. We have here the factor that has everywhere more than any other prompted the fiercest opposition to the 'philosophic' God of mere rational speculation, who can be put into a definition. And for their part the philosophers have condemned these expressions of the energy of the numen,

---

1. Compare, too, the experience on p. 70: '. . . What I felt on these occasions was a temporary loss of my own identity.'
2. The *mobilitas Dei* of Lactantius.

whenever they are brought on to the scene, as sheer anthropomorphism. In so far as their opponents have for the most part themselves failed to recognize that the terms they have borrowed from the sphere of human conative and affective life have merely value as analogies, the philosophers are right to condemn them. But they are wrong, in so far as, this error notwithstanding, these terms stood for a genuine aspect of the divine nature – its non-rational aspect – a due consciousness of which served to protect religion itself from being 'rationalized' away.

For wherever men have been contending for the 'living' God or for voluntarism, there, we may be sure, have been non-rationalists fighting rationalists and rationalism. It was so with Luther in his controversy with Erasmus; and Luther's *omnipotentia Dei* in his *De Servo Arbitrio* is nothing but the union of 'majesty' – in the sense of absolute supremacy – with this 'energy', in the sense of a force that knows not stint nor stay, which is urgent, active, compelling, and alive. In mysticism, too, this element of 'energy' is a very living and vigorous factor, at any rate in the 'voluntaristic' mysticism, the mysticism of love, where it is very forcibly seen in that 'consuming fire' of love whose burning strength the mystic can hardly bear, but begs that the heat that has scorched him may be mitigated, lest he be himself destroyed by it. And in this urgency and pressure the mystic's 'love' claims a perceptible kinship with the ὀργή itself, the scorching and consuming wrath of God; it is the same 'energy', only differently directed. 'Love', says one of the mystics, 'is nothing else than quenched wrath.'

The element of 'energy' reappears in Fichte's speculations on the Absolute as the gigantic, never-resting, active world-stress, and in Schopenhauer's daemonic 'Will'. At the same time both these writers are guilty of the same error that is already found in myth; they transfer 'natural' attributes, which ought only to be used as 'ideograms' for what is itself properly beyond utterance, to the non-rational as real qualifications of it, and they mistake symbolic expressions of feelings for adequate concepts upon which a 'scientific' structure of knowledge may be based.

In Goethe, as we shall see later, the same element of energy is emphasized in a quite unique way in his strange descriptions of the experience he calls 'daemonic'.

THE ANALYSIS OF 'MYSTERIUM'

Ein begriffener Gott ist kein Gott.
'A God comprehended is no God.'

TERSTEEGEN

We gave to the object to which the numinous consciousness is directed the name *mysterium tremendum*, and we then set ourselves first to determine the meaning of the adjective *tremendum* – which we found to be itself only justified by analogy – because it is more easily analysed than the substantive idea *mysterium*. We have now to turn to this, and try, as best we may, by hint and suggestion, to get to a clearer apprehension of what it implies.

The 'Wholly Other'

It might be thought that the adjective itself gives an explanation of the substantive; but this is not so. It is not merely analytical; it is a synthetic attribute to it; i.e. *tremendum* adds something not necessarily inherent in *mysterium*. It is true that the reactions in consciousness that correspond to the one readily and spontaneously overflow into those that correspond to the other; in fact, anyone sensitive to the use of words would commonly feel that the idea of 'mystery' (*mysterium*) is so closely bound up with its synthetic qualifying attribute 'aweful' (*tremendum*) that one can hardly say the former without catching an echo of the latter, 'mystery' almost of itself becoming 'aweful mystery' to us. But the passage from the one idea to the other need not by any means be always so easy. The elements of meaning implied in 'awefulness' and 'mysteriousness' are in themselves definitely different. The latter may so far preponderate in the religious consciousness, may stand out so vividly, that in comparison with it the former almost sinks out of sight;

a case which again could be clearly exemplified from some forms of mysticism. Occasionally, on the other hand, the reverse happens, and the *tremendum* may in turn occupy the mind without the *mysterium*.

This latter, then, needs special consideration on its own account. We need an expression for the mental reaction peculiar to it; and here, too, only one word seems appropriate, though, as it is strictly applicable only to a 'natural' state of mind, it has here meaning only by analogy: it is the word 'stupor'. *Stupor* is plainly a different thing from *tremor*; it signifies blank wonder, an astonishment that strikes us dumb, amazement absolute.[1] Taken, indeed, in its purely natural sense, *mysterium* would first mean merely a secret or a mystery in the sense of that which is alien to us, uncomprehended and unexplained; and so far *mysterium* is itself merely an ideogram, an analogical notion taken from the natural sphere, illustrating, but incapable of exhaustively rendering, our real meaning. Taken in the religious sense, that which is 'mysterious' is – to give it perhaps the most striking expression – the 'wholly other' (θάτερον, *anyad, alienum*), that which is quite beyond the sphere of the usual, the intelligible, and the familiar, which therefore falls quite outside the limits of the 'canny', and is contrasted with it, filling the mind with blank wonder and astonishment.

This is already to be observed on the lowest and earliest level of the religion of primitive man, where the numinous consciousness is but an inchoate stirring of the feelings. What is really characteristic of this stage is *not* – as the theory of Animism would have us believe – that men are here concerned

1. Compare also *obstupefacere*. Still more exact equivalents are the Greek θάμβος and θαμβεῖν. The sound θ α μ β (*thamb*) excellently depicts this state of mind of blank, staring wonder. And the difference between the moments of *stupor* and *tremor* is very finely suggested by the passage, Mark x. 32 (cf. *infra*, p. 175). On the other hand, what was said above of the facility and rapidity with which the two moments merge and blend is also markedly true of θάμβος which then becomes a classical term for the (ennobled) awe of the numinous in general. So Mark xvi. 5 is rightly translated by Luther 'und sie entsetzten sich', and by the English Authorized Version 'and they were affrighted'.

with curious entities, called 'souls' or 'spirits', which happen to be invisible. Representations of spirits and similar conceptions are rather one and all early modes of 'rationalizing' a precedent experience, to which they are subsidiary. They are attempts in some way or other – it little matters how – to guess the riddle it propounds, and their effect is at the same time always to weaken and deaden the experience itself. They are the source from which springs, not religion, but the rationalization of religion, which often ends by constructing such a massive structure of theory and such a plausible fabric of interpretation that the 'mystery' is frankly excluded.[1] Both imaginative 'myth', when developed into a system, and intellectualist Scholasticism, when worked out to its completion, are methods by which the fundamental fact of religious experience is, as it were, simply rolled out so thin and flat as to be finally eliminated altogether.

Even on the lowest level of religious development the essential characteristic is therefore to be sought elsewhere than in the appearance of 'spirit' representations. It lies rather, we repeat, in a peculiar 'moment' of consciousness, to wit, the *stupor* before something 'wholly other', whether such an other be named 'spirit' or 'daemon' or 'deva', or be left without any name. Nor does it make any difference in this respect whether, to interpret and preserve their apprehension of this 'other', men coin imagery of their own or adapt imaginations drawn from the world of legend, the fabrications of fancy apart from and prior to any stirrings of daemonic dread.

In accordance with laws of which we shall have to speak again later, this feeling or consciousness of the 'wholly other' will attach itself to, or sometimes be indirectly aroused by means of, objects which are already puzzling upon the 'natural' plane, or are of a surprising or astounding character; such as extraordinary phenomena or astonishing occurrences or things in inanimate nature, in the animal world, or among men. But here once more we are dealing with a case of association

1. A spirit or soul that has been conceived and comprehended no longer prompts to 'shuddering', as is proved by Spiritualism. But it thereby ceases to be of interest for the psychology of religion.

between things specifically different – the 'numinous' and the 'natural' moments of consciousness – and not merely with the gradual enhancement of one of them – the 'natural' – till it becomes the other. As in the case of 'natural fear' and 'daemonic dread' already considered, so here the transition from natural to daemonic amazement is not a mere matter of degree. But it is only with the latter that the complementary expression *mysterium* perfectly harmonizes, as will be felt perhaps more clearly in the case of the adjectival form 'mysterious'. No one says, strictly and in earnest, of a piece of clockwork that is beyond his grasp, or of a science that he cannot understand: 'That is "mysterious" to me.'

It might be objected that the mysterious is something which is and remains absolutely and invariably beyond our understanding, whereas that which merely eludes our understanding for a time but is perfectly intelligible in principle should be called, not a 'mystery', but merely a 'problem'. But this is by no means an adequate account of the matter. The truly 'mysterious' object is beyond our apprehension and comprehension, not only because our knowledge has certain irremovable limits, but because in it we come upon something inherently 'wholly other', whose kind and character are incommensurable with our own, and before which we therefore recoil in a wonder that strikes us chill and numb.[1]

This may be made still clearer by a consideration of that degraded offshoot and travesty of the genuine 'numinous' dread or awe, the fear of ghosts. Let us try to analyse this experience. We have already specified the peculiar feeling-element of 'dread' aroused by the ghost as that of 'grue', grisly horror.[2]

---

1. In *Confessions*, ii. 9. 1, Augustine very strikingly suggests this stiffening, benumbing element of the 'wholly other' and its contrast to the rational aspect of the numen; the *dissimile* and the *simile*:

'Quid est illud, quod interlucet mihi et percutit cor meum sine laesione? Et inhorresco et inardesco. *Inhorresco*, in quantum *dissimilis* ei sum. Inardesco, in quantum similis ei sum.'

('What is that which gleams through me and smites my heart without wounding it? I am both a-shudder and a-glow. A-shudder, in so far as I am unlike it, a-glow in so far as I am like it.')

2. *gruseln, gräsen.*

Now this 'grue' obviously contributes something to the attraction which ghost-stories exercise, in so far, namely as the relaxation of tension ensuing upon our release from it relieves the mind in a pleasant and agreeable way. So far, however, it is not really the ghost itself that gives us pleasure, but the fact that we are rid of it. But obviously this is quite insufficient to explain the ensnaring attraction of the ghost-story. The ghost's real attraction rather consists in this, that of itself and in an uncommon degree it entices the imagination, awakening strong interest and curiosity; it is the weird thing itself that allures the fancy. But it does this, not because it is 'something long and white' (as someone once defined a ghost), nor yet through any of the positive and conceptual attributes which fancies about ghosts have invented, but because it is a thing that 'doesn't really exist at all', the 'wholly other', something which has no place in our scheme of reality but belongs to an absolutely different one, and which at the same time arouses an irrepressible interest in the mind.

But that which is perceptibly true in the fear of ghosts, which is after all only a caricature of the genuine thing, is in a far stronger sense true of the 'daemonic' experience itself, of which the fear of ghosts is a mere offshoot. And while, following this main line of development, this element in the numinous consciousness, the feeling of the 'wholly other', is heightened and clarified, its higher modes of manifestation come into being, which set the numinous object in contrast not only to everything wonted and familiar (i.e. in the end, to nature in general), thereby turning it into the 'super-natural', but finally to the world itself, and thereby exalt it to the 'supramundane', that which is above the whole world-order.

In mysticism we have in the 'beyond' ($\epsilon\pi\epsilon\kappa\epsilon\iota\nu\alpha$) again the strongest stressing and over-stressing of those non-rational elements which are already inherent in all religion. Mysticism continues to its extreme point this contrasting of the numinous object (the numen), as the 'wholly other', with ordinary experience. Not content with contrasting it with all that is of nature or this world, mysticism concludes by contrasting it with Being itself and all that 'is', and finally actually calls it 'that which is nothing'. By this 'nothing' is meant not only that of which nothing can be predicated, but that which is absolutely and intrinsically other than and opposite of everything that is and can be thought. But while exaggerating to the point of paradox this *negation* and contrast – the only means open to conceptual thought to apprehend the *mysterium* – mysticism at the same time retains the *positive quality* of the 'wholly other' as a very living factor in its over-brimming religious emotion.

But what is true of the strange 'nothingness' of our mystics holds good equally of the *sūnyam* and the *sūnyatā*, the 'void' and 'emptiness' of the Buddhist mystics. This aspiration for the 'void' and for becoming void, no less than the aspiration of our Western mystics for 'nothing' and for becoming nothing, must seem a kind of lunacy to anyone who has no inner sympathy for the esoteric language and ideograms of mysticism, and lacks the matrix from which these come necessarily to birth. To such an one Buddhism itself will be simply a morbid sort of pessimism. But in fact the 'void' of the Eastern, like the 'nothing' of the Western, mystic is a numinous ideogram of the 'wholly other'.

These terms 'supernatural' and 'transcendent'[1] give the appearance of positive attributes, and, as applied to the mysterious, they appear to divest the *mysterium* of its originally negative meaning and to turn it into an affirmation. On the side of conceptual thought this is nothing more than appearance, for it is obvious that the two terms in question are merely negative and exclusive attributes with reference to 'nature' and the world or cosmos respectively. But on the side of the feeling-content it is otherwise; that *is* in very truth positive in the highest degree, though here too, as before, it cannot be rendered explicit in conceptual terms. It is through this positive feeling-content that the concepts of the 'transcendent' and 'supernatural' become forthwith designations for a unique 'wholly other' reality and quality, something of whose special character we can *feel*, without being able to give it clear conceptual expression.

1. Literally, supramundane: *überweltlich*.

'Mysterium Tremendum'

The Element of Fascination

The qualitative *content* of the numinous experience, to which 'the mysterious' stands as *form*, is in one of its aspects the element of daunting 'awefulness' and 'majesty', which has already been dealt with in detail; but it is clear that it has at the same time another aspect, in which it shows itself as something uniquely attractive and *fascinating*.

These two qualities, the daunting and the fascinating, now combine in a strange harmony of contrasts, and the resultant dual character of the numinous consciousness, to which the entire religious development bears witness, at any rate from the level of the 'daemonic dread' onwards, is at once the strangest and most noteworthy phenomenon in the whole history of religion. The daemonic-divine object may appear to the mind an object of horror and dread, but at the same time it is no less something that allures with a potent charm, and the creature, who trembles before it, utterly cowed and cast down, has always at the same time the impulse to turn to it, nay even to make it somehow his own. The 'mystery' is for him not merely something to be wondered at but something that entrances him; and beside that in it which bewilders and confounds, he feels a something that captivates and transports him with a strange ravishment, rising often enough to the pitch of dizzy intoxication; it is the Dionysiac-element in the numen.

The ideas and concepts which are the parallels or 'schemata' on the rational side of this non-rational element of 'fascination' are love, mercy, pity, comfort; these are all 'natural' elements of the common psychical life, only they are here thought of as absolute and complete. But important as these are for the experience of religious bliss or felicity, they do not by any means exhaust it. It is just the same as with the opposite experience of religious infelicity – the experience of the ὀργή or 'wrath' of God – both alike contain fundamentally non-rational elements. Bliss or beatitude is more, far more, than the mere natural feeling of being comforted, of reliance, of the joy of love, however these may be heightened and enhanced. Just as 'wrath', taken in a purely rational or a purely ethical sense, does not exhaust that profound element of *awefulness* which is locked in the mystery of deity, so neither does 'graciousness' exhaust the profound element of *wonderfulness* and rapture which lies in the mysterious beatific experience of deity. The term 'grace' may indeed be taken as its aptest designation, but then only in the sense in which it is really applied in the language of the mystics, and in which not only the 'gracious intent' but 'something more' is meant by the word. This 'something more' has its antecedent phases very far back in the history of religions.

It may well be possible, it is even probable, that in the first stage of its development the religious consciousness started with only one of its poles – the 'daunting' aspect of the numen – and so at first took shape only as 'daemonic dread'. But if this did not point to something beyond itself, if it were not but one 'moment' of a completer experience, pressing up gradually into consciousness, then no transition would be possible to the feelings of positive self-surrender to the numen. The only type of worship that could result from this 'dread' alone would be that of ἀπαιτεῖσθαι and ἀποτρέπειν, taking the form of expiation and propitiation, the averting or the appeasement of the 'wrath' of the numen. It can never explain how it is that 'the numinous' is the object of search and desire and yearning, and that too for its own sake and not only for the sake of the aid and backing that men expect from it in the natural sphere. It can never explain how this takes place, not only in the forms of 'rational' religious worship, but in those queer 'sacramental' observances and rituals and procedures of communion in which the human being seeks to get the numen into his possession.

Religious practice may manifest itself in those normal and easily intelligible forms which occupy so prominent a place in the history of religion, such forms as propitiation, petition, sacrifice, thanksgiving, etc. But besides these there is a series of strange proceedings which are constantly attracting greater and greater attention, and in which it is claimed that we may recognize, besides mere religion in general, the particular roots of mysticism. I refer to those numerous curious modes of behaviour and fantastic forms of mediation, by means of which the primitive religious man attempts to master 'the mysterious', and to fill himself and even to identify himself with it. These modes of behaviour fall apart into two classes. On the one hand the 'magical' identification of the self with the numen proceeds by means of various transactions, at once magical and devotional in character – by formula, ordination, adjuration, consecration, exorcism, etc.: on the other hand are the 'shamanistic' ways of procedure, possession, indwelling, self-fulfilment in exaltation and ecstasy. All these have, indeed, their starting-points simply in magic, and their intention at first was certainly simply to appropriate the prodigious force of the numen for the natural ends of man. But the process does not rest there. Possession of and by the numen becomes an end in itself; it begins to be sought for its own sake; and the wildest and most artificial methods of asceticism are put into practice to attain it. In a word, the *vita religiosa* begins; and to remain in these strange and bizarre states of numinous possession becomes a good in itself, even a way of salvation, wholly different from the profane goods pursued by means of magic. Here, too, commences the process of development by which the experience is matured and purified, till finally it reaches its consummation in the sublimest and purest states of the 'life within the Spirit' and in the noblest mysticism. Widely various as these states are in themselves, yet they have this element in common, that in them the *mysterium* is experienced in its essential, positive, and specific character, as something that bestows upon man a beatitude beyond compare, but one whose real nature he can neither proclaim in speech nor conceive in thought, but may know only by a direct and living experience. It is a bliss which embraces all those blessings that are indicated or suggested in positive fashion by any 'doctrine of salvation', and it quickens all of them through and through; but these do not exhaust it. Rather by its all-pervading, penetrating glow it makes of these very blessings more than the intellect can conceive in them or affirm of them. It gives the peace that passes understanding, and of which the tongue can only stammer brokenly. Only from afar, by metaphors and analogies, do we come to apprehend what it is in itself, and even so our notion is but inadequate and confused.

'Eye hath not seen, nor ear heard, neither have entered into the heart of man, the things which God hath prepared for them that love him.' Who does not feel the exalted sound of these words and the 'Dionysiac' element of transport and fervour in them? It is instructive that in such phrases as these, in which consciousness would fain put its highest consummation into words, 'all images fall away' and the mind turns from them to grasp expressions that are purely negative. And it is still more instructive that in reading and hearing such words their merely negative character simply is not noticed; that we can let whole chains of such negations enrapture, even intoxicate us, and that entire hymns – and deeply impressive hymns – have been composed, in which there is really nothing positive at all! All this teaches us the independence of the positive content of this experience from the implications of its overt conceptual expression, and how it can be firmly grasped, thoroughly understood, and profoundly appreciated, purely in, with, and from the feeling itself.

Mere love, mere trust, for all the glory and happiness they bring, do not explain to us that moment of rapture that breathes in our tenderest and most heart-felt hymns of salvation, as also in such eschatological hymns of longing as that Rhyme of St Bernard in which the very verses seem to dance.

Urbs Sion unica, mansio mystica, condita coelo,
Nunc tibi gaudeo, nunc tibi lugeo, tristor, anhelo,
Te, quia corpore non queo, pectore saepe penetro;
Sed caro terrea, terraque carnea, mox cado retro.
Nemo retexere, nemoque promere sustinet ore,
Quo tua moenia, quo capitolia plena nitore.
Id queo dicere, quo modo tangere pollice coelum,
Ut mare currere, sicut in aere figere telum.
Opprimit omne cor ille tuus decor, O Sion, O Pax.
Urbs sine tempore, nulla potest fore laus tibi mendax.

O nova mansio, te pia concio, gens pia munit,
Provehit, excitat, auget, identitat, efficit, unit.[1]

This is where the living 'something more' of the *fascinans*, the element of fascination, is to be found. It lives no less in those tense extollings of the blessing of salvation, which recur in all religions of salvation, and stand in such remarkable contrast to the relatively meagre and frequently childish import of that which is revealed in them by concept or by image. Everywhere salvation is something whose meaning is often very little apparent, is even wholly obscure, to the 'natural' man; on the contrary, *so far as he understands it*, he tends to find it highly tedious and uninteresting, sometimes downright distasteful and repugnant to his nature, as he would, for instance, find the beatific vision of God in our own doctrine of salvation, or the *henōsis* of 'God all in all' among the mystics. 'So far as he understands', be it noted; but then he does not understand it in the least. Because he lacks the inward teaching of the Spirit, he must needs confound what is offered him as an expression for the experience of salvation – a mere ideogram of what is felt, whose import it hints at by analogy – with 'natural' concepts, as though it were itself just such an one. And so he 'wanders ever farther from the goal'.

It is not only in the religious feeling of longing that the moment of fascination is a living factor. It is already alive and present in the moment of 'solemnity', both in the gathered concentration and humble submergence of private devotion, when the mind is exalted to the holy, and in the common

1. 'O Sion, thou city sole and single, mystic mansion hidden away in the heavens, now I rejoice in thee, now I moan for thee and mourn and yearn for thee; thee often I pass through in the heart, as I cannot in the body, but being but earthly flesh and fleshly earth soon I fall back. None can disclose or utter in speech what plenary radiance fills thy walls and thy citadels. I can as little tell of it as I can touch the skies with my finger, or run upon the sea or make a dart stand still in the air. This thy splendour overwhelms every heart, O Sion, O Peace! O timeless City, no praise can belie thee. O new dwelling-place, thee the concourse and people of the faithful erects and exalts, inspires and increases, joins to itself, and makes complete and one.'

worship of the congregation, where this is practised with earnestness and deep sincerity, as, it is to be feared, is with us a thing rather desired than realized. It is this and nothing else that in the solemn moment can fill the soul so full and keep it so inexpressibly tranquil. Schleiermacher's assertion[1] is perhaps true of it, as of the numinous consciousness in general, viz. that it cannot really occur alone on its own account, or except combined and penetrated with rational elements. But, if this be admitted, it is upon other grounds than those adduced by Schleiermacher; while, on the other hand, it may occupy a more or less predominant place and lead to states of calm (ἡσυχία) as well as of transport, in which it *almost* of itself wholly fills the soul. But in all the manifold forms in which it is aroused in us, whether in eschatological promise of the coming kingdom of God and the transcendent bliss of Paradise, or in the guise of an entry into that beatific reality that is 'above the world'; whether it come first in expectancy or pre-intimation or in a present experience ('When I but *have* Thee, I ask no question of heaven and earth'); in all these forms, outwardly diverse but inwardly akin, it appears as a strange and mighty propulsion towards an ideal good known only to religion and in its nature fundamentally non-rational, which the mind knows of in yearning and presentiment, recognizing it for what it is behind the obscure and inadequate symbols which are its only expression. And this shows that above and beyond our rational being lies hidden the ultimate and highest part of our nature, which can find no satisfaction in the mere allaying of the needs of our sensuous, psychical, or intellectual impulses and cravings. The mystics called it the basis or ground of the soul.

We saw that in the case of the element of the mysterious the 'wholly other' led on to the supernatural and transcendent and that above these appeared the 'beyond' (ἐπέκεινα) of mysticism, through the non-rational side of religion being raised to its highest power and stressed to excess. It is the same in the case of the element of 'fascination'; here, too, is possible a transition into mysticism. At its highest point of

1. *Glaubenslehre*, § 5.

50

stress the fascinating becomes the 'overabounding', exuberant',[1] the mystical 'moment' which exactly corresponds upon
this line to the ἐπέκεινα upon the other line of approach, and
which is to be understood accordingly. But while this feeling
of the 'over-abounding' is specially characteristic of mysticism,
a trace of it survives in all truly felt states of religious beatitude,
however restrained and kept within measure by other factors.
This is seen most clearly from the psychology of those great
experiences – of grace, conversion, second birth – in which the
religious experience appears in its pure intrinsic nature and in
heightened activity, so as to be more clearly grasped than in
the less typical form of piety instilled by education. The hard
core of such experiences in their Christian form consists of the
redemption from guilt and bondage to sin, and we shall have
presently to see that this also does not occur without a parti-
cipation of non-rational elements. But leaving this out of
account, what we have here to point out is the unutterableness
of what has been yet genuinely experienced, and how such an
experience may pass into blissful excitement, rapture, and exaltation verging often on the bizarre and the abnormal.[2] This is
vouched for by the autobiographical testimony of the 'con-
verted' from St Paul onward. William James has collected a
great number of these, without, however, himself noticing the
non-rational element that thrills in them.

Thus, one writes

> ... For the moment nothing but an ineffable joy and exaltation
> remained. It is impossible fully to describe the experience. It was
> like the effect of some great orchestra, when all the separate notes
> have melted into one swelling harmony, that leaves the listener

1. *das Überschwengliche.*
2. This may be found fatal to the attempt to construct a 'religion
within the limits of pure reason', or 'of humanity'; but none the less
the matter is as we have described it, as far as concerns the psychological inquiry into religion, which asks, not what it is within the
aforementioned limits, but what it is in its own essential nature. And
for that matter this proceeding of constructing a 'humanity' prior to
and apart from the most central and potent of human capacities is
like nothing so much as the attempt to frame a standard idea of the
human body after having previously cut off the head.

conscious of nothing save that his soul is being wafted upwards and almost bursting with its own emotion. (*Varieties of Religious Experience*, p. 66.)

And another:

... The more I seek words to express this intimate intercourse, the more I feel the impossibility of describing the thing by any of our usual images. (Ibid., p. 68.)

And almost with the precision of dogma, a third (Jonathan Edwards) indicates the qualitative difference of the experience of beatitude from other 'rational' joy:

The conceptions which the saints have of the loveliness of God and that kind of delight which they experience in it are quite peculiar and entirely different from anything which a natural man can possess or of which he can form any proper notion. (Ibid., p. 229.)

Cf. also pp. 192, 225; and the testimony of Jacob Boehme given on p. 417. Also this of Boehme:

But I can neither write nor tell of what sort of Exaltation the triumphing in the Spirit is. It can be compared with nought, but that when in the midst of death life is born, and it is like the resurrection of the dead.

With the mystics these experiences pass up wholly into the 'over-abounding'. 'O that I could tell you what the heart feels, how it burns and is consumed inwardly! Only, I find no words to express it. I can but say: Might but one little drop of what I feel fall into Hell, Hell would be transformed into a Paradise.' So says St Catherine of Genoa; and all the multitude of her spiritual kindred testify to the same effect.

What we Christians know as the experiences of grace and the second birth have their parallels also in the religions of high spiritual rank beyond the borders of Christianity. Such are the breaking out of the saving 'Bodhi', the opening of the 'heavenly eye', the *Jñāna*, by *Iśvaras prasāda*, which is victorious over the darkness of nescience and shines out in an experience with which no other can be measured. And in all these the entirely non-rational and specific element in the beatific experience is immediately noticeable. The qualitative character of it varies widely in all these cases, and is again in them all very different from its parallels in Christianity; still in all it is very similar in intensity, and in all it is a 'salvation' and an absolute 'fascination', which in contrast to all that admits of 'natural' expression or comparison is deeply imbued with the 'over-abounding' ('exuberant') nature of the numen.

And this is also entirely true of the rapture of Nirvana, which is only in appearance a cold and negative state. It is only conceptually that 'Nirvana' is a negation; it is felt in consciousness as in the strongest degree positive; it exercises a 'fascination' by which its votaries are as much carried away as are the Hindu or the Christian by the corresponding objects of their worship. I recall vividly a conversation I had with a Buddhist monk. He had been putting before me methodically and pertinaciously the arguments for the Buddhist 'theology of negation', the doctrine of Anātman and 'entire emptiness'. When he had made an end, I asked him, what then Nirvana itself is; and after a long pause came at last the single answer, low and restrained: 'Bliss – unspeakable'. And the hushed restraint of that answer, the solemnity of his voice, demeanour, and gesture, made more clear what was meant than the words themselves.

And so we maintain, on the one hand, following the *via eminentiae et causalitatis*, that the divine is indeed the highest, strongest, best, loveliest, and dearest that man can think of; but we assert on the other, following the *via negationis*, that God is not *merely* the ground and superlative of all that can be thought; He is in Himself a subject on His own account and in Himself.

*

In the adjective δεινός the Greek language possesses a word peculiarly difficult to translate, and standing for an idea peculiarly difficult to grasp in all its strange variations. And if we ask whence this difficulty arises, the answer is plain; it is because δεινός is simply the numinous (mostly of course at a lower level, in an arrested form, attenuated by rhetorical or poetic usage). Consequently δεινός is the equivalent of *dirus* and *tremendus*. It may mean evil or imposing, potent and strange, queer and marvellous, horrifying and fascinating, divine and daemonic, and a source of 'energy'. Sophocles means to awaken the feeling of 'numinous awe' through the whole gamut of its phases at the contemplation of man, the creature of marvel, in the choric song of the *Antigone*:

πολλὰ τὰ δεινά, κοὐδὲν ἀνθρώπου δεινότερον πέλει.

This line defies translation, just because our language has no term that can isolate distinctly and gather into one word the total numinous impression a thing may make on the mind. The nearest that German can get to it is in the expression *das Ungeheuere* (monstrous), while in English 'weird' is perhaps the closest rendering possible. The mood and attitude represented in the foregoing verse might then be fairly well rendered by such a translation as:

Much there is that is weird; but nought is weirder than man.

The German *ungeheuer* is not by derivation simply 'huge', in quantity or quality; – this, its common meaning, is in fact a rationalizing interpretation of the real idea; it is that which is not *geheuer*, i.e. approximately, the *uncanny* – in a word, the numinous. And it is just this element of the uncanny in man that Sophocles has in mind. If this, its fundamental meaning, be really and thoroughly felt in consciousness, then the word could be taken as a fairly exact expression for the numinous in its aspects of mystery, awefulness, majesty, augustness, and 'energy'; nay, even the aspect of fascination is dimly felt in it.

The variations of meaning in the German word *ungeheuer* can be well illustrated from Goethe.[1] He, too, uses the word first to denote the huge in size – what is too vast for our faculty of space-perception, such as the immeasurable vault of the night sky. In other passages the word retains its original non-rational colour more markedly; it comes to mean the uncanny,

1. Cf. *Wilhelm Meisters Wanderjahre*, Bk. I, ch. 10; *Wahlverwandtschaften*, 2. 15; *Dichtung und Wahrheit*, 2. 9: 4. 20.

the fearful, the dauntingly 'other' and incomprehensible, that which arouses in us *stupor* and θάμβος; and finally, in the wonderful words of Faust which I have put at the beginning of this book, it becomes an almost exact synonym for our 'numinous' under all its aspects.

> Das Schaudern ist der Menschheit bestes Teil.
> Wie auch die Welt ihm das Gefühl verteuere,
> Ergriffen fühlt er tief das Ungeheuere.[1]

1. Awe is the best of man: howe'er the world's
   Misprizing of the feeling would prevent us,
   Deeply we feel, once gripped, the weird Portentous.
   (GOETHE, *Faust*, Second Part, Act 1, Sc. v.)

CHAPTER V

Analogies and Associated Feelings

In order to give an adequate account of this second aspect of the numinous, we were led to add to its original designation as *mysterium tremendum* that it at the same time exercises a supreme 'fascination'. And this its dual character, as at once an object of boundless awe and boundless wonder, quelling and yet entrancing the soul, constitutes the proper *positive* content of the *mysterium* as it manifests itself in conscious feeling. No attempt of ours to describe this harmony of contrasts in the import of the *mysterium* can really succeed; but it may perhaps be adumbrated, as it were from a distance, by taking an analogy from a region belonging not to religion but to aesthetics. In the category and feeling of the *sublime* we have a counterpart to it, though it is true it is but a pale reflection, and moreover involves difficulties of analysis all its own. The analogies between the consciousness of the sublime and of the numinous may be easily grasped.[1] To begin with, 'the sublime', like 'the numinous', is in Kantian language an idea or concept 'that cannot be unfolded' or explicated (*unauswickelbar*). Certainly we can tabulate some general 'rational' signs that uniformly recur as soon as we call an object sublime; as, for instance, that it must approach, or threaten to overpass, the bounds of our understanding by some 'dynamic' or 'mathematic' greatness, by potent manifestations of force or magnitude in spatial extent. But these are obviously only conditions of, not the essence of, the impression of sublimity. A thing does not

1. We are often prone to resort to this familiar feeling-content to fill out the negative concept 'transcendent', explaining frankly God's 'transcendence' by His 'sublimity'. As a figurative analogical description this is perfectly allowable, but it would be an error if we meant it literally and in earnest. Religious feelings are not the same as aesthetic feelings, and 'the sublime' is as definitely an aesthetic term as 'the beautiful', however widely different may be the facts denoted by the words.

become sublime merely by being great. The concept itself remains unexplicated; it has in it something mysterious, and in this it is like that of the numinous. A second point of resemblance is that the sublime exhibits the same peculiar dual character as the numinous; it is at once daunting, and yet again singularly attracting, in its impress upon the mind. It humbles and at the same time exalts us, circumscribes and extends us beyond ourselves, on the one hand releasing in us a feeling analogous to fear, and on the other rejoicing us. So the idea of the sublime is closely similar to that of the numinous, and is well adapted to excite it and to be excited by it, while each tends to pass over into the other.

THE LAW OF THE ASSOCIATION OF FEELINGS

As these expressions 'excite' and 'pass over' will later assume importance, and as the latter in particular is hedged about with misconceptions which are prominent in the modern doctrines of Evolution and give rise to quite erroneous conclusions, we will enter at once upon a closer consideration of them.

It is a well known and fundamental psychological law that ideas 'attract' one another, and that one will excite another and call it into consciousness, if it resembles it. An entirely similar law holds good with regard to feelings. A feeling, no less than an idea, can arouse its like in the mind; and the presence of the one in my consciousness may be the occasion for my entertaining the other at the same time. Further, just as in the case of ideas the law of reproduction by similarity leads to a mistaken substitution of ideas, so that I come to entertain an idea x, when y would have been the appropriate one, so we may be led to a corresponding substitution of feelings, and I may react with a feeling x to an impression to which the feeling y would normally correspond. Finally, *I* can pass from one feeling to another by an imperceptibly gradual transition, the one feeling x dying away little by little, while the other, y, excited together with it, increases and strengthens in a corresponding degree. But it is important here to recognize the true account of the phenomenon. What passes over – undergoes transition – is not the feeling itself. It is not that the actual feeling gradually changes in quality or 'evolves', i.e. transmutes itself into a quite different one, but rather that *I* pass over or make the transition from one feeling to another as my circumstances change, by the gradual decrease of the one and increase of the other. A transition of the actual feeling into another would be a real 'transmutation', and would be a psychological counterpart to the alchemist's production of gold by the transmutation of metals.

And yet it is this transmutation that is assumed by the modern 'Evolutionism' – more properly to be called 'Transmutationism' – by the introduction of the equivocal phrase, 'gradually evolve' (i.e. from a thing of a certain quality to something qualitatively different), or the no less equivocal words 'Epigenesis', 'Heterogony',[1] and their like. In this way, they would have us believe, the feeling, e.g. of moral obligation, 'evolves' or develops. At first, so it is said, all that exists is the simple constraint of uniform custom, as seen in the community of the clan. Then, out of that, it is said, 'arises' the idea of a universally obligatory 'ought'. How the idea can do so is not disclosed. Now such a theory misses the fact that in moral obligation we have something *qualitatively* quite different from constraint by custom. The finer and more penetrating psychological analysis that can apprehend differences in quality is rudely ignored and in consequence the whole problem is misconceived. Or, if something of the essential difference is felt, it is covered up and glozed over by the phrase 'gradually evolve', and the one thing is made to turn into the other *par la durée*, much as milk grows sour from standing. But 'ought' is a primary and unique meaning, as little derivable from another as blue from bitter, and there are not 'transmutations' in the psychological any more than in the physical world. The idea 'ought' is only 'evolvable' out of the spirit of man itself, and then in the sense of being 'arousable', because it is already

1. Neither Heterogony nor Epigenesis is genuine Evolution. They are rather just what the biologists call *generatio equivoca*, and therefore mere formation of an aggregate by addition and accumulation.

potentially implanted in him. Were it not so, no 'evolution' could effect an introduction for it.

The evolutionists may be quite correct in reconstructing the kind of historical process that took place, viz. the gradual and successive entry upon the scene of different 'moments' of feeling-consciousness in historical sequence, and the order of entry itself may have been correctly discovered. But the explanation of this process is quite different from that which they intend; it is, namely, the law of the excitation and arousing of feelings and ideas according to the measure of their resemblance. There is in point of fact a very strong analogy between constraint by custom and constraint by moral obligation, as both are constraints upon conduct. Consequently the former can *arouse* the latter in the mind if it – the latter – was already potentially planted there; the feeling of 'ought' may start into consciousness at the presence of the other feeling, and the man may gradually effect a transition to it from that other. But what we are concerned with is the *replacement* of the one by the other, and not the *transmutation* of the one into the other.

Now it is just the same with the feeling of the numinous as with that of moral obligation. It too is not to be derived from any other feeling, and is in this sense 'unevolvable'. It is a content of feeling that is qualitatively *sui generis*, yet at the same time one that has numerous analogies with others, and therefore it and they may reciprocally excite or stimulate one another and cause one another to appear in the mind. Instead of framing 'epigenetic' and other fabrications of the course the evolution of religion has taken, it is our task to inquire into these 'stimuli' or 'excitations', these elements that cause the numinous feeling to appear in consciousness, to intimate by virtue of what analogies they came to be able to do so, and so to discover the series or chain of these stimuli by whose operation the numinous feeling was awakened in us.

Such a power of stimulation characterizes the feeling of the sublime, in accordance with the law we found, and through the analogies it bears to the numinous feeling. But this is indubitably a stimulus that only makes its appearance late in the excitation-series, and it is probable that the feeling of the sublime is itself first aroused and disengaged by the precedent religious feeling – not from itself, but from the rational spirit of man and its *a priori* capacity.

SCHEMATIZATION

The 'association of ideas' does not simply cause the idea *y* to reappear in consciousness with the given idea *x* occasionally only, it also sets up under certain circumstances lasting combinations and connexions between the two. And this is no less true of the association of feelings. Accordingly we see religious feeling in permanent connexion with other feelings which are conjoined to it in accordance with this principle of association. It is, indeed, more accurate to say 'conjoined' than really 'connected', for such mere conjunctions or chance connexions according to laws of purely external analogy are to be distinguished from necessary connexions according to principles of true inward affinity and cohesion. An instance of a connexion of this latter kind – an example, indeed, of an inner *a priori* principle – is (following the theory of Kant) the connexion of the category of causality with its temporal 'schema', the temporal sequence of two successive events, which by being brought into connexion with the category of causality is *known* and recognized as a causal relation of the two. In this case analogy between the two – the category and the schema – has also a place, but it is not chance external resemblance but essential correspondence, and the fact that the two belong together is here a necessity of our reason. On the basis of such a necessity the temporal sequence 'schematizes' the category.

Now the relation of the rational to the non-rational element in the idea of the holy or sacred is just such a one of 'schematization', and the non-rational numinous fact, schematized by the rational concepts we have suggested above, yields us the complex category of 'holy' itself, richly charged and complete and in its fullest meaning. And that the schematism is a genuine one, and not a mere combination of analogies, may be distinctly seen from the fact that it does not fall to pieces, and cannot be cut out as the development of the consciousness of religious truth proceeds onwards and upwards, but is only recognized with greater definiteness and certainty. And it is for the same reason inherently probable that there is more, too, in the combination of 'the holy' with 'the sublime' than a mere association of feelings; and perhaps we may say that, while as a matter of historical genesis such an association was the means whereby this combination was awakened in the mind and the occasion for it, yet the inward and lasting character of the connexion in all the higher religions does prove that 'the sublime' too is an authentic 'schema' of 'the holy'.

The intimate interpenetration of the non-rational with the rational elements of the religious consciousness, like the interweaving of warp and woof in a fabric, may be elucidated by taking another familiar case, in which a universal human feeling, that of personal affection, is similarly interpenetrated by a likewise thoroughly non-rational and separate element, namely, the sex instinct. It goes without saying that this latter lies just on the opposite side of 'reason' to the numinous consciousness; for, while this is 'above all reason', the sex impulse is below it, an element in our instinctive life. 'The numinous' infuses the rational from above, 'the sexual' presses up from beneath, quite wholesomely and normally out of the nature which the human being shares with the general animal world, into the higher realm of the specifically 'humane'. But though the two things I am comparing are thus manifestly opposite extremes, they have a closely corresponding relation to that which lies between them, viz. the reason. For the quite special domain of the 'erotic' is only brought into existence as the reproductive instinct passes up out of the merely instinctive life, penetrates the higher humane life of mind and feeling, and infuses wishes, cravings, and longings in personal liking, friendship, and love, in song and poetry and imaginative creation in general. Whatever falls within the sphere of the erotic is therefore always a composite product, made up of two factors: the one something that occurs also in the general sphere of human behaviour as such, as friendship and liking, the feeling of companionship, the mood of poetic inspiration or joyful exaltation, and the like; and the other an infusion of a quite special kind, which is not to be classed with these, and of which no one can have any inkling, let alone understand it, who has not learnt from the actual inward experience of *erōs* or love. Another point in which the 'erotic' is analogous to the 'holy' is in having in the main no means of linguistic expression but terms drawn from other fields of mental life, which only cease to be 'innocuous' (i.e. only become genuinely 'erotic' terms) when it is realized that the lover, like the orator, bard, or singer, expresses himself not so much by the actual words he uses as by the accent, tone, and imitative gesture which reinforce them.

The phrase 'he loves me' is verbally identical, whether it is said by a child of its father or by a girl of her lover. But in the second case a 'love' is meant which is at the same time 'something more' (viz. *sexual* love), and something more not only in quantity but in quality. So, too, the phrase 'We ought to fear, love, and trust him'[1] is verbally identical, whether it refers to the relation of child to father or to that of man to God. But again in the second case these ideas are infused with a meaning of which none but the religious-minded man can have any comprehension or indeed any inkling, whose presence makes, e.g. the 'fear of God' 'something more' than any fear of a man, qualitatively, not merely quantitatively, though retaining the essence of the most genuine reverence felt by the child for its father. And Suso means in the same way to distinguish 'love' and 'love of God', when he says:

There was never a string so dulcet-toned but ceased to sound if stretched to a withered frame; a heart poor in love can no more understand speech rich in love than a German can an Italian.[2]

There is another kind of experience in which we may find an example of the way in which rational elements in our feeling-consciousness may be thus penetrated by quite non-rational ones, and an example even more proximate to the complex feeling of the holy than that just described – 'erotic'

1. Luther's amplification of the First Commandment.
2. *Works*, ed. Denifle, p. 309.

experience – in so far as the non-rational element is, like the numinous feeling but unlike the sexual impulse, at the same time *supra*-rational. I refer to the state of mind induced in us by a song set to music. The verbal text of the song expresses feelings that are 'natural', homesickness perhaps, or confidence in time of danger, hope for a future good, or joy in a present possession – all concrete elements in our 'natural' human lot, and capable of being described in conceptual terms. But it is otherwise with the music, purely as music. It releases a blissful rejoicing in us, and we are conscious of a glimmering, billowy agitation occupying our minds, without being able to express or explain in concepts what it really is that moves us so deeply. And to say that the music is mournful or exultant, that it incites or restrains, is merely to use signs by analogy, choosing them for their resemblance to the matter in hand out of other regions of our mental life; and at any rate we cannot say what the object or ground of this mourning or exulting may be. Music, in short, arouses in us an experience and vibrations of mood that are quite specific in kind and must simply be called 'musical'; but the rise and fall and manifold variations of this experience exhibit – though again only in part – definite, if fugitive, analogies and correspondences with our ordinary non-musical emotional states, and so can call these into consciousness and blend with them. If this happens, the specific 'music-consciousness' is thereby 'schematized' and rationalized, and the resultant complex mood is, as it were, a fabric, in which the general human feelings and emotional states constitute the warp, and the non-rational music-feelings the woof. The song in its entirety is therefore music 'rationalized'.

Now here is illustrated the contrast between the legitimate and the illegitimate processes of 'rationalization'. For, if the song may be called music 'rationalized' in the legitimate sense, in programme-music we have a musical 'rationalism' in the bad sense. Programme-music, that is to say, misinterprets and perverts the idea of music by its implication that the inner content of music is not – as in fact it is – something unique and mysterious, but just the incidental experiences – joy and grief, expansion and repression – familiar to the human heart. And in its attempt to make of musical tones a language to recount the fortunes of men, programme-music abolishes the autonomy of music, and is deceived by a mere resemblance into employing as a means what is an end and substantive content in its own right. It is just the same mistake as when the 'august' aspect of the numinous is allowed to evaporate into the 'morally good', instead of merely being 'schematized' by it, or as when we let 'the holy' be identified with 'the perfectly good' will. And not only programme-music is at fault here. The 'music-drama' of Wagner, by attempting a thoroughgoing unification of the musical and the dramatic, commits the same offence against both the non-rational spirit of the former and the autonomy of either. We can only succeed in very partial and fragmentary fashion in 'schematizing' the non-rational factor in music by means of the familiar incidents of human experience. And the reason is just this, that the real content of music is not drawn from the ordinary human emotions at all, and that it is in no way merely a second language, alongside the usual one, by which these emotions find expression. Musical feeling is rather (like numinous feeling) something 'wholly other', which, while it affords analogies and here and there will run parallel to the ordinary emotions of life, cannot be made to coincide with them by a detailed point-to-point correspondence. It is, of course, from those places where the correspondence holds that the spell of a composed song arises by a blending of verbal and musical expression. But the very fact that we attribute to it a spell, an enchantment, points in itself to that 'woof' in the fabric of music of which we spoke, the woof of the unconceived and non-rational.[1]

But we must beware of confounding in any way the non-rational of music and the non-rational of the numinous itself, as Schopenhauer, for example, does. Each is something in its own right, independently of the other. We shall discuss later whether, and how far, the former may become a means of expression for the latter.

[1]. This is the point of view from which to estimate both the excellent and the inadequate features of E. Hanslick's book, *Vom Musikalisch-Schönen*.

CHAPTER VI

The Holy as a Category of Value

SIN AND ATONEMENT

WE have already met that strange and profound mental reaction to the numinous which we proposed to call 'creature-feeling' or creature-consciousness, with its concomitant feelings of submergence and prostration and of the diminution of the self into nothingness; bearing always in mind that these expressions do not hit with precision, but merely hint at what is really meant,[1] inasmuch as this 'diminution of the self', etc., is something very different from the littleness, weakness, or dependence of which we may become aware under other conditions than that of numinous feeling. And we had to notice that this experience marks a definite depreciation or disvaluation of the self in respect, so to speak, of its reality and very existence. We have now to put alongside of this another sort of self-disvaluation, which has long been a matter of common observation, and only needs to be suggested in order to be recognized. 'I am a man of *unclean* lips and dwell among a people of unclean lips.' 'Depart from me, for I am a *sinful* man, O Lord.' So say respectively Isaiah and Peter, when the numinous reality encounters them as a present fact of consciousness. In both cases this self-depreciating feeling-response is marked by an immediate, almost instinctive, spontaneity. It is not based on deliberation, nor does it follow any rule, but breaks, as it were, palpitant from the soul – like a direct reflex movement at the stimulation of the numinous. It does not spring from the consciousness of some committed transgression, but rather is an immediate datum given with the feeling of the numen: it proceeds to 'disvalue' together with the

1. Cf. Hugo of St Victor's words: 'Sumpta sunt vocabula, ut intellegi aliquatenus posset quod comprehendi non poterat.' ('These words were chosen, that that which could not be comprehended might yet in some measure be understood.')

self the tribe to which the person belongs, and indeed, together with that, all existence in general. Now it is to-day pretty generally agreed that, all this being the case, these outbursts of feeling are not simply, and probably at first not at all, *moral* depreciations, but belong to a quite special category of valuation and appraisement. The feeling is beyond question not that of the transgression of the moral law, however evident it may be that such a transgression, where it has occurred, will involve it as a consequence: it is the feeling of absolute 'profaneness'.

But what is this? Again something which the 'natural' man cannot, as such, know or even imagine. He, only, who is 'in the Spirit' knows and feels what this 'profaneness' is; but to such an one it comes with piercing acuteness, and is accompanied by the most uncompromising judgement of self-depreciation, a judgement passed, not upon his character, because of individual 'profane' actions of his, but upon his own very existence as creature before that which is supreme above all creatures. And at the same moment he passes upon the numen a judgement of *appreciation* of a unique kind by the category diametrically contrary to 'the profane', the category 'holy', which is proper to the numen alone, but to it is in an absolute degree; he says: '*Tu solus sanctus*'. This '*sanctus*' is not merely 'perfect' or 'beautiful' or 'sublime' or 'good', though, being like these concepts also a *value*, objective and ultimate, it has a definite, perceptible analogy with them. It is the positive *numinous* value or worth, and to it corresponds on the side of the creature a numinous *disvalue* or 'unworth'.

In every highly-developed religion the appreciation of moral obligation and duty, ranking as a claim of the deity upon man, has been developed side by side with the religious feeling itself. None the less a profoundly humble and heartfelt recognition of 'the holy' may occur in particular experiences without being always or definitely charged or infused with the sense of moral demands. The 'holy' will then be recognized as that which commands our respect, as that whose real value is to be acknowledged inwardly. It is not that the awe of holiness is itself simply 'fear' in face of what is absolutely overpowering, before which there is no alternative to blind, awe-struck obedience. '*Tu solus sanctus*' is rather a paean of *praise*, which, so far from being merely a faltering confession of the divine supremacy, recognizes and extols a value, precious beyond all conceiving. The object of such praise is not simply absolute might, making its claims and compelling their fulfilment, but a might that has at the same time the supremest *right* to make the highest claim to service, and receives praise because it is in an absolute sense worthy to be praised. 'Thou art *worthy* . . . to receive glory and honour and power' (Rev. iv. 11).

When once it has been grasped that *qādôsh* or *sanctus* is not originally a *moral* category at all, the most obvious rendering of the words is 'transcendent' ('supramundane', *überweltlich*). The one-sided character of this rendering to which we had to take exception has been supplemented by the more detailed exposition of the numinous and its implications. But its most essential defect remains to be noted: 'transcendent' is a purely ontological attribute and not an attribute of *value*; it denotes a character that can, if need be, abash us, but cannot inspire us with *respect*. It might once again, therefore, be an advantage to introduce another term to underline this side of the numinous, and the words *augustus* and σεμνός suggest themselves for the purpose. *Augustus*, 'august', no less than σεμνός, is really appropriate only to numinous objects – to rulers only as offspring or descendants of gods. Then, while σεβαστός indicates the *being* of the numen, σεμνός or *augustus* would refer rather to its supreme worth or *value*, its illustriousness. There will, then, in fact be two values to distinguish in the numen; its 'fascination' (*fascinans*) will be that element in it whereby it is of *subjective* value (= beatitude) to man; but it is 'august' (*augustum*) in so far as it is recognized as possessing in itself *objective* value that claims our homage.

Mere 'unlawfulness' only becomes 'sin', 'impiety', 'sacrilege', when the character of *numinous unworthiness* or *disvalue* goes on to be transferred to and centred in *moral* delinquency. And only when the mind feels it as 'sin' does the transgression of law become a matter of such dreadful gravity for the conscience, a catastrophe that leads it to despair of its own power. The meaning of 'sin' is not understood by the 'natural', nor even by the merely moral, man; and the theory of certain dogmatists, that the demand of morality as such urged man on to an inner collapse and then obliged him to look round for some deliverance, is palpably incorrect. There are serious-minded men of sincere moral endeavour who cannot understand what such a 'deliverance' or 'redemption' may be, and dismiss it with a shrug of the shoulders. They are aware that they are erring and imperfect men, but they know and put into practice the methods of self-discipline, and so labour onward upon their way with sturdy resolution. The morally robust older rationalism was lacking neither in a sincere and respectful recognition of the moral law nor in honest endeavour to conform to it. It knew well and sternly condemned what was 'wrong', and the aim of its exhortations and instruction was that men should realize better and take more in earnest the facts of moral right and wrong. But no 'downfall' or 'collapse' and no 'need of redemption' came within its scheme, because the objection brought against it by its opponents was in fact just; rationalism lacked understanding of what 'sin' is.[1] Mere morality is not the soil from which grows either the need of 'redemption' and deliverance or the need for that other unique good which is likewise altogether and specifically numinous in character, 'covering', and 'atonement'. There would perhaps be less disputing as to the warrant and value of these latter in

---

1. Cf. the testimony of Theodore Parker – certainly a man of far from crude mental development – as to his own experience, given by W. James. *Varieties*, p. 81:

'They (*sc.* the heathen of classical antiquity) were conscious of wrath, of cruelty, avarice, drunkenness, lust, sloth, cowardice, and other actual vices, and struggled and got rid of the deformities; but they were not conscious of "enmity against God" and didn't sit down and whine and groan against non-existent evil. I have done wrong things enough in my life, and do them now: I miss the mark, draw bow, and try again. But . . . I know there is much "health in me"; and in my body, even now, there dwelleth many a good thing, spite of consumption and Saint Paul.'

If there is nothing crude about such a statement, it is at any rate *superficial*. The depths of the non-rational consciousness must be stirred to find with Anselm 'quanti ponderis sit peccatum'.

Christian doctrine if dogmatic theology itself had not transferred them from their mystical sphere into that of rational
ethics and attenuated them into moral concepts. They were
thus taken from a sphere where they have an authentic and
necessary place to one where their validity is most disputable.

We meet the 'moment' of 'covering' in specially clear form
in the religion of Yahweh, in its rites and the emotion they
excite; but it is contained also, though more obscurely, in
many other religions. It comprises, first, a manifestation of
the numinous awe, viz. the feeling that the 'profane' creature
cannot forthwith approach the numen, but has need of a
covering or shield against the ὀργή of the numen. Such a
'covering' is then a 'consecration', i.e. a procedure that renders
the approacher himself 'numinous', frees him from his 'profane' being, and fits him for intercourse with the numen. The
means of 'consecration', however – 'means of grace' in the
proper sense – are derived from, or conferred and appointed by,
the numen itself, which bestows something of its own quality
to make man capable of communion with it. And this act is
something very different from the 'annulment of mistrust', the
phrase in which Ritschl seeks to rationalize these relations
between God and man.

'Atonement', following our view, is a 'sheltering' or 'covering', but a profounder form of it. It springs directly from the
idea of numinous value or worth and numinous disvalue or
unworth as soon as these have been developed. Mere awe,
mere need of shelter from the *tremendum*, has here been elevated to the feeling that man in his 'profaneness' is not *worthy*
to stand in the presence of the holy one, and that his own
entire personal unworthiness might defile even holiness itself.
This is obviously the case in the vision of the call of Isaiah;
and the same note recurs, less emphatically but quite unmistakably, in the story of the centurion of Capernaum (Luke vii.
1–10), and his words: 'I am not worthy that thou shouldest
enter under my roof.' Here we have both the light thrill of awe
before the *tremendum* of the numen and also, and more
especially, the feeling of this unique disvalue or unworth of the
profane confronted by the numen, which suggests to the man

that even holiness itself may be tainted and tarnished by his presence.

Here, then, comes in the felt necessity and longing for 'atonement', and all the more strongly when the close presence of the numen, intercourse with it, and enduring possession of it, becomes an object of craving, is even desired as the *summum bonum*. It amounts to a longing to transcend this sundering unworthiness, given with the self's existence as 'creature' and profane natural being. It is an element in the religious consciousness, which so far from vanishing in the measure in which religion is deepened and heightened, grows on the contrary continually stronger and more marked. Belonging, as it does, wholly to the non-rational side of religion, it may remain latent while, in the course of religious evolution, the rational side at first unfolds and assumes vigorous and definite form; it may retire for a time behind other elements and apparently die away, but only to return more powerfully and insistently than before. And again it may grow to be the sole, one-sided, exclusive interest, a cry that drowns all other notes, so that the religious consciousness is distorted and disfigured; as may readily happen where through long periods of time the rational aspects of religion have been fostered unduly and at the cost of the non-rational.

The special character of this consciousness of need for atonement may perhaps be brought home more clearly by an analogy from our 'natural' emotional life; but at the same time it is important that the religious feeling we are considering should itself be kept distinct from its analogue, as the two are frequently confounded. The analogy is with the feeling arising from moral transgression. There, too, we practise a kind of self-depreciation which is clear and familiar and perfectly intelligible to us, when we esteem ourselves *guilty* of a bad action and the action itself as morally evil. The evil of the action *weighs upon us* and deprives us of our self-respect. We *accuse* ourselves and *remorse* sets in. But alongside this self-depreciation stands a second one, which while it may have reference to the same action as the other yet avails itself of definitely different categories. The same perverse action that before weighed upon us now *pollutes* us; we do not accuse ourselves, we are defiled in our own eyes. And the characteristic form of emotional reaction is no longer remorse but *loathing*. The man feels a need, to express which he has recourse to images of *washing* and cleansing. The two kinds of self-depreciation proceed on parallel lines and may relate to the same action; but none the less it is obvious that they are, inwardly and in their essence, determinately different. Now the second of them has a plain analogy with the need for 'atonement', and so can fairly be drawn upon for its elucidation; while at the same time it is yet nothing more than an analogy from another sphere, viz. that of morality.

No religion has brought the mystery of the need for atonement or expiation to so complete, so profound, or so powerful expression as Christianity. And in this, too, it shows its superiority over others. It is a more perfect religion and more perfectly religion than they, in so far as what is potential in religion in general becomes in Christianity a pure actuality. And the distrust and suspicion which so widely obtains with regard to this mystery is only to be explained from the general custom – for which our theoretical cult of homiletics, liturgy, and catechism is largely responsible – of taking into account only the rational side of religion. Yet this atonement mystery is a 'moment' which no Christian teaching that purports to represent the religious experience of the Christian and Biblical tradition can afford to surrender. The teacher will have to make explicit, by an analysis of the Christian religious experience, how the 'very numen', by imparting itself to the worshipper, becomes itself the means of 'atonement'. And in this regard it does not matter so very much what the decisions of the commentators are as to what, if anything, St Paul or St Peter wrote on the subject of expiation and atonement, or whether, indeed, there is any 'scriptural authority' for the thing at all. Were there in scripture no word written about it, it might still be written to-day from our own experience. But it would indeed be extraordinary if it had not long ago been written of. For the God of the New Testament is not less holy than the God of the Old Testament, but more holy. The interval between the creature and Him is not diminished but made absolute; the unworthiness of the profane in contrast to Him is not extenuated but enhanced. That God none the less admits access to Himself and intimacy with Himself is not a mere matter of course; it is a grace beyond our power to apprehend, a prodigious paradox. To take this paradox out of Christianity is to make it shallow and superficial beyond recognition. But if this is so, the intuitions concerning, and the need felt for, 'covering' and 'atonement' result immediately. And the divinely appointed means of God's self-revelation, where experienced and appraised as such – 'the Word', 'the Spirit', 'the Person of Christ' – become that to which the man 'flees', in which he finds refuge, and in which he 'hides' himself, in order that, consecrated and cleansed of his 'profaneness' thereby, he may come into the presence of Holiness itself.

That these ideas are viewed with a certain distrust may be traced to two causes. One is that what is a specifically religious element is distortingly moralized. If we start from mere morality and in relation to a God understood as being the personification of the moral order endowed with love, then all these things are wholly inapplicable and a source of genuine difficulty. But we are concerned with *religious* (not merely moral) intuitions, and it is impossible to dispute how right or wrong they are with a man whose interest is wholly in morality and not in religion, and who is therefore quite incapable of appreciating them. Whoever, on the other hand, penetrates to the unique centre of the religious experience, so that it starts awake in his own consciousness, finds that the truth of these intuitions is experienced directly, as soon as he penetrates into their depths.

The other ground of distrust is that usually in our theological systems an attempt is made to develop conceptual *theories* of these ideas, which are all pure intuitions, emotional rather than conceptual in character. They are thus made objects of speculation, and the final outcome is the quasi-mathematical 'doctrine of imputation' and its drastic ascription to the credit of the 'sinner' of the 'merit' of Christ, not to mention the learned inquiry whether this transaction involves an 'analytic' or a 'synthetic' judgement of God.

*

Let us look back once more from the point we have reached over the course our inquiry has so far taken. As the subtitle of this book suggests, we were to investigate the non-rational element in the idea of the divine. The words 'non-rational' and 'irrational' are to-day used almost at random. The non-rational is sought over the most widely different regions, and writers generally shirk the trouble of putting down precisely what they intend by the term, giving it often the most multifarious meaning or applying it with such vague generality that it admits of the most diverse interpretations. Pure fact in contrast to law, the empirical in contrast to reason, the contingent in contrast to the necessary, the psychological in contrast to transcendental fact, that which is known *a posteriori* in contrast to that which is determinable *a priori*; power, will, and arbitrary choice in contrast to reason, knowledge, and determination by value; impulse, instinct, and the obscure forces of the subconscious in contrast to insight, reflection, and intelligible plan; mystical depths and stirrings in the soul, surmise, presentiment, intuition, prophecy, and finally the 'occult' powers also; or, in general, the uneasy stress and universal fermentation of the time, with its groping after the thing never yet heard or seen in poetry of the plastic arts – all these and more may claim the names 'non-rational', 'irrational', and according to circumstances are extolled or condemned as modern 'irrationalism'. Whoever makes use of the word 'non-rational' to-day ought to say what he actually means by it. This we did in our introductory chapter. We began with the 'rational' in the idea of God and the divine, meaning by the term that in it which is clearly to be grasped by our power of conceiving, and enters the domain of familiar and definable conceptions. We went on to maintain that beneath this sphere of clarity and lucidity lies a hidden depth, inaccessible to our conceptual thought, which we in so far call the 'non-rational'.

The meaning of the two contrasted terms may be made

plainer by an illustration. A deep joy may fill our minds without any clear realization upon our part of its source and the object to which it refers, though some such objective reference there must always be. But as attention is directed to it the obscure object becomes clearly identified in precise conceptual terms. Such an object cannot, then, be called, in our sense of the word, 'non-rational'. But it is quite otherwise with religious 'bliss' and its essentially numinous aspect, the *fascinans*. Not the most concentrated attention can elucidate the object to which this state of mind refers, bringing it out of the impenetrable obscurity of feeling into the domain of the conceptual understanding. It remains purely a felt experience, only to be indicated symbolically by 'ideograms'. That is what we mean by saying it is non-rational.

And the same is true of all the moments of the numinous experience. The consciousness of a 'wholly other' evades precise formulation in words, and we have to employ symbolic phrases which seem sometimes sheer paradox, that is, *ir*-rational, not merely non-rational, in import. So with religious awe and reverence. In ordinary fear and in moral reverence I can indicate in conceptual terms what it is that I fear or revere; injury, e.g., or ruin in the one case, heroism or strength of character in the other. But the object of *religious* awe or reverence – the *tremendum* and *augustum*, cannot be fully determined conceptually: it is non-rational, as is the beauty of a musical composition, which no less eludes complete conceptual analysis.

Confronted by the fact of the non-rational thus interpreted we cannot be satisfied with a mere bare statement, which would open the door to all the vague and arbitrary phraseology of an emotionalist irrationalism. We are bound to try, by means of the most precise and unambiguous symbolic and figurative terms that we can find, to discriminate the different elements of the experience so far as we can in a way that can claim general validity.

CHAPTER VII

Means of Expression of the Numinous

DIRECT MEANS

IT may serve to make the essential nature of the numinous consciousness clearer if we call to mind the manner in which it expresses itself outwardly, and how it spreads and is transmitted from mind to mind. There is, of course, no 'transmission' of it in the proper sense of the word; it cannot be 'taught', it must be 'awakened' from the spirit. And this could not justly be asserted, as it often is, of religion as a whole and in general, for in religion there *is* very much that *can* be taught – that is, handed down in concepts and passed on in school instruction. What is incapable of being so handed down is this numinous basis and background to religion, which can only be induced, incited, and aroused. This is least of all possible by mere verbal phrase or external symbol; rather we must have recourse to the way all other moods and feelings are transmitted, to a penetrative imaginative sympathy with what passes in the other person's mind. More of the experience lives in reverent attitude and gesture, in tone and voice and demeanour, expressing its momentousness, and in the solemn devotional assembly of a congregation at prayer, than in all the phrases and negative nomenclature which we have found to designate it. Indeed, these never give a positive suggestion of the object to which the religious consciousness refers; they are only of assistance in so far as they profess to indicate *an* object, which they at the same time contrast with another, at once distinct from and inferior to it, e.g. 'the invisible', 'the eternal' (non-temporal), 'the supernatural', 'the transcendent'. Or they are simply ideograms for the unique content of feeling, ideograms to understand which a man must already have had the experience himself. Far the best means are actual 'holy' situations or their representation in description. If a man does not *feel* what the numinous is, when he reads the sixth chapter of Isaiah, then no 'preaching, singing, telling', in Luther's phrase, can avail him. Little of it can usually be noticed in theory and dogma, or even in exhortation, unless it is actually *heard*. Indeed no element in religion needs so much as this the *viva vox*, transmission by living fellowship and the inspiration of personal contact.[1]

But the mere word, even when it comes as a living voice, is powerless without the 'spirit in the heart' of the hearer to move him to apprehension. And this spirit, this inborn capacity to receive and understand, is the essential thing. If that is there, very often only a very small incitement, a very remote stimulus, is needed to arouse the numinous consciousness. It is indeed astonishing to see how small a stimulus suffices – and that too coming sometimes only in clumsy and bewildered guise – to raise the spirit of itself to the strongest pitch of the most definitely religious excitement. But where the wind of the spirit blows, there the mere 'rational' terms themselves are indued with power to arouse the feeling of the 'non-rational', and become adequate to tune the mood at once to the right tone. Here 'schematization' starts at once and needs no prompting. He who 'in the spirit' reads the written word lives in the numinous, though he may have neither notion of it nor name for it, nay, though he may be unable to analyse any feeling of his own and so make explicit to himself the nature of that numinous strand running through the religious experience.

INDIRECT MEANS

For the rest, the methods by which the numinous feeling is presented and evoked are indirect; i.e. they consist in those means by which we express kindred and similar feelings belonging to the 'natural' sphere. We have already become acquainted with these feelings, and we shall recognize them at once if we consider what are the means of expression which religion has employed in all ages and in every land.

1. Suso says of the transmission of the mystical experience: 'One thing there may be known; unlike as it is, when a man heareth himself a dulcet instrument of strings sweetly sounding, compared to whoso

One of the most primitive of these – which is later more and more felt to be inadequate, until it is finally altogether discarded as 'unworthy' – is quite naturally the 'fearful' and horrible, and even at times the revolting and the loathsome. Inasmuch as the corresponding feelings are closely analogous to that of the *tremendum*, their outlets and means of expression may become indirect modes of expressing the specific 'numinous awe' that cannot be expressed directly. And so it comes about that the horrible and dreadful character of primitive images and pictures of gods, which seems to us to-day frequently so repellent, has even yet among naïve and primitive natures – nay, occasionally even among ourselves – the effect of arousing genuine feelings of authentic religious awe. And, vice versa, this awe operates as a supremely potent stimulus to express the element of terror in different forms of imaginative representation. The hard, stern, and somewhat grim pictures of the Madonna in ancient Byzantine art attract the worship of many Catholics more than the tender charm of the Madonnas of Raphael. This trait is most signally evident in the case of certain figures of gods in the Indian pantheon. Durgā, the 'great Mother' of Bengal, whose worship can appear steeped in an atmosphere of profoundest devotional awe, is represented in the orthodox tradition with the visage of a fiend. And this same blending of appalling frightfulness and most exalted holiness can perhaps be even more clearly studied in the eleventh chapter of the Bhagavad-Gītā,[1] in which Vishnu – who is yet to his votaries the very principle of goodness – displays himself to Aryuna in the true height of his divinity. Here, too, the mind has recourse for mode of expression first to the fearful

but heareth tell thereof, even so are the words which are received in the purity of grace and flow forth out of a living heart by a living mouth unlike to those same words if they are beheld upon the dead parchment. . . . For there they grow cold, I know not how, and wither away like roses that have been plucked. For the lovely melody that above all toucheth the heart is then quenched to silence; and in the waste places of the withered heart are they then received.'

1. Nowhere can the non-rational element of ὀργή be better studied than in this chapter, one of the perfectly classical passages for the theory of Religion.

and dreadful, though this is at the same time permeated with that element of 'the grand' to which we next turn.

This mode of expression, by way of 'grandeur' or 'sublimity', is found on higher levels, where it replaces mere 'terror' and 'dread'. We meet it in an unsurpassable form in the sixth chapter of Isaiah, where there is sublimity alike in the lofty throne and the sovereign figure of God, the skirts of His raiment 'filling the temple' and the solemn majesty of the attendant angels about Him. While the element of 'dread' is gradually overborne, the connexion of 'the sublime' and 'the holy' becomes firmly established as a legitimate schematization and is carried on into the highest forms of religious consciousness – a proof that there exists a hidden kinship between the numinous and the sublime which is something more than a merely accidental analogy, and to which Kant's *Critique of Judgement* bears distant witness.

So far we have been concerned with that element or factor of the numinous which was the first our analysis noted and which we proposed to name symbolically 'the aweful' (*tremendum*). We pass now to consider the means by which the second – the element of 'the mysterious' (*mysterium*) – is expressed. Here we light upon the analogical mode of manifestation that in every religion occupies a foremost and extraordinary place, and the theory of which we are now in a position to give. I refer to *miracle*. 'Miracle is the dearest child of Faith'; if the history of religions had not already taught us the truth of Schiller's saying, we might have reached it by anticipation *a priori* from the element of 'the mysterious', as already shown. Nothing can be found in all the world of 'natural' feelings bearing so immediate an analogy – *mutatis mutandis* – to the religious consciousness of ineffable, unutterable mystery, the 'absolute other', as the incomprehensible, unwonted, enigmatic thing, in whatever place or guise it may confront us. This will be all the more true if the uncomprehended thing is something at once *mighty* and *fearful*, for then there is a twofold analogy with the numinous – that is to say, an analogy not only with the *mysterium* aspect of it, but with the *tremendum* aspect, and latter again in the two directions already suggested of *fearfulness* proper and *sublimity*. This exemplifies the general truth already considered that any form of the numinous consciousness may be stirred by means of feelings analogous to it of a 'natural' kind, and then itself pass over into these, or, more properly, be replaced by them. And, in fact, this is everywhere manifest in the experience of man. Whatever has loomed upon the world of his ordinary concerns as something terrifying and baffling to the intellect; whatever among natural occurrences or events in the human, animal, or vegetable kingdoms has set him a-stare in wonder and astonishment – such things have ever aroused in man, and become endued with, the 'daemonic dread' and numinous feeling, so as to become 'portents', 'prodigies', and 'marvels'. Thus and only thus is it that 'the miraculous' rose. And, in the reverse direction, the feeling of the *numen* as 'the mysterious' worked as a potent stimulus on the naïve imagination, inciting it to expect miracles, to invent them, to 'experience' them, to recount them, just as before the felt awefulness of the numen became a stimulus to select or fashion inventively, as a means of religious expression, images of fear and dread. 'The mysterious' became an untiring impulse, prompting to inexhaustible invention in folk-tale and myth, saga and legend, permeating ritual and the forms of worship, and remaining till to-day to naïve minds, whether in the form of narrative or sacrament, the most powerful factor that keeps the religious consciousness alive. But here too, as in the case of the fearful and terrible, progress to a higher stage of development shows the gradual elimination of this merely external analogue to the numinous, viz. the miraculous; and so we see how, on the more enlightened levels, 'miracle' begins to fade away; how Christ is at one with Mohammed and Buddha in declining the role of mere wonder-worker; how Luther dismisses the 'outward miracles' disparagingly as 'jugglery' or 'apples and nuts for children'; and finally how the 'supernaturalism' of miracle is purged from religion as something that is only an imperfect analogue and no genuine 'schema' of the numinous.

There are other manifestations of this tendency of the feeling of the 'mysterious' to be attracted to objects and aspects of experience analogous to it in being 'uncomprehended'. It finds its most unqualified expression in the spell exercised by the only half intelligible or wholly unintelligible language of devotion, and in the unquestionably real enhancement of the awe of the worshipper which this produces. Instances of this are – the ancient traditional expressions, still retained despite their obscurity, in our Bible and hymnals; the special emotional virtue attaching to words like 'Hallelujah', *Kyrie eleison*, 'Selah', just because they are 'wholly other' and convey no clear meaning; the Latin in the service of the Mass, felt by the Catholic to be, not a necessary evil, but something especially holy; the Sanskrit in the Buddhist Mass of China and Japan; the 'language of the gods' in the ritual of sacrifice in Homer; and many similar cases. Especially noticeable in this connexion are the half-revealed, half-concealed elements in the service of the Mass, in the Greek Church liturgy, and so many others; we can see here one factor that justifies and warrants them. And the same is true of the remaining portions of the old Mass which recur in the Lutheran ritual. Just because their design shows but little of regularity or conceptual arrangement, they preserve in themselves far more of the spirit of worship than the proposed recastings of the service put forward by the most recent practical reformers. In these we find carefully arranged schemes worked out with the balance and coherence of an essay, but nothing unaccountable, and for that very reason suggestive; nothing accidental, and for that very reason pregnant in meaning; nothing that rises from the deeps below consciousness to break the rounded unity of the wonted disposition, and thereby point to a unity of a higher order – in a word, little that is really spiritual. All the cases cited, then, derive their power of suggestion from the same source; they are all instances of the analogy to 'the mysterious' afforded by that which is not wholly understood, unwonted and at the same time venerable through age; and in the resemblance they present to the 'mysterious' they arouse it in the mind by a sort of 'anamnēsis' or reminder, and at the same time constitute its outward analogical representation.

MEANS BY WHICH THE NUMINOUS IS EXPRESSED IN ART

In the arts nearly everywhere the most effective means of representing the numinous is 'the sublime'. This is especially true of architecture, in which it would appear to have first been realized. One can hardly escape the idea that this feeling for expression must have begun to awaken far back in the remote Megalithic Age. The motive underlying the erection of those gigantic blocks of rock, hewn or unworked, single monoliths or titanic rings of stone, as at Stonehenge, may have well been originally to localize and preserve and, as it were, to store up the numen in solid presence by magic; but the change to the motive of *expression* must have been from the outset far too vividly stimulated not to occur at a very early date. In fact the bare feeling for solemn and imposing magnitude and for the pomp of sublime pose and gesture is a fairly elementary one, and we cannot doubt that this stage had been reached when the *mastabas*, obelisks, and pyramids were built in Egypt. It is indeed beyond question that the builders of these temples, and of the Sphinx of Gizeh, which set the feeling of the sublime, and together with and through it that of the numinous, throbbing in the soul almost like a mechanical reflex, must themselves have been conscious of this effect and have intended it.

Further, we often say of a building, or indeed of a song, a formula, a succession of gestures or musical notes, and in particular of certain manifestations of ornamental and decorative art, symbols, and emblems, that they make a 'downright magical' impression, and we feel we can detect the special characteristic of this 'magical' note in art with fair assurance even under the most varying conditions and in the most diverse relationships. The art of China, Japan, and Tibet, whose specific character has been determined by Taoism and Buddhism, surpasses all others in the unusual richness and depth of such impressions of the 'magical', and even an inexpert observer responds to them readily. The designation 'magical' is here correct even from the historical point of view, since the origin of this language of form was properly magical representations, emblems, formularies, and contrivances. But the actual impression of 'magic' is quite independent of this historical bond of connexion with magical practices. It occurs even when nothing is known of the latter; nay, in that case it comes out most strongly and unbrokenly. Beyond dispute art has here a means of creating a unique impression – that of the magical – apart from and independent of reflection. Now the magical is nothing but a suppressed and dimmed form of the numinous, a crude form of it which great art purifies and ennobles. In great art the point is reached at which we may no longer speak of the 'magical', but rather are confronted with the numinous itself, with all its impelling motive power, transcending reason, expressed in sweeping lines and rhythm.[1] In no art, perhaps, is this more fully realized than in the great landscape painting and religious painting of China in the classical period of the T'ang and Sung dynasties. It has been said of this great art:

These works are to be classed with the profoundest and sublimest of the creations of human art. The spectator who, as it were, immerses himself in them feels behind these waters and clouds and mountains the mysterious breath of the primeval Tao, the pulse of innermost being. Many a mystery lies half-concealed and half-revealed in these pictures. They contain the knowledge of the 'nothingness' and the 'void', of the 'Tao' of heaven and earth, which is also the Tao of the human heart. And so, despite

1. This numinous–magical character is specially noticeable in the strangely impressive figures of the Buddha in early Chinese art; and here too it affects the observer independently of 'ideas', i.e. without his knowing anything about the speculative doctrines of Buddhism. Thus Sirén justly says of the great Buddha from the Lung-Men Caves (T'ang Dynasty):

'Anyone who approaches this figure will realize that it has a religious significance without knowing anything about its *motif*. . . . It matters little whether we call it a prophet or a god, because it is a complete work of art permeated by a spiritual will, which communicates itself to the beholder. . . . The religious element of such a figure is immanent; it is "a presence" or an atmosphere rather than a formulated idea. . . . It cannot be described in words, because it lies beyond intellectual definition.'

(Oswald Sirén, *Chinese Sculpture*, London, 1925, vol. i, p. 20.)

their perpetual agitation, they seem as remotely distant and as profoundly calm as though they drew secret breath at the bottom of a sea.[1]

To us of the West the Gothic appears as the most numinous of all types of art. This is due in the first place to its sublimity; but Worringer in his work, *Probleme der Gothik*, has done a real service in showing that the peculiar impressiveness of Gothic does not consist in its sublimity alone, but draws upon a strain inherited from primitive magic, of which he tries to show the historical derivation. To Worringer, then, the impression Gothic makes is one of magic; and, whatever may be said of his historical account of the matter, it is certain that in this at least he is on the right track. Gothic *does* instil a spell that is more than the effect of sublimity. But 'magic' is too low a word: the tower of the Cathedral of Ulm is emphatically not 'magical', it is *numinous*. And the difference between the numinous and the merely magical can nowhere be felt more clearly than in the splendid plate Worringer gives in his book of this marvellous work of architecture. But when this is said, we may still keep the word 'magic' in use to denote the style and means of artistic expression by which the impression of the numinous comes into being.

But in neither the sublime nor the magical, effective as they are, has art more than an indirect means of representing the numinous. Of directer methods our Western art has only two, and they are in a noteworthy way *negative*, viz. *darkness* and *silence*. The darkness must be such as is enhanced and made all the more perceptible by contrast with some last vestige of brightness, which it is, as it were, on the point of extinguishing; hence the 'mystical' effect begins with semi-darkness. Its impression is rendered complete if the factor of the 'sublime' comes to unite with and supplement it. The semi-darkness that glimmers in vaulted halls, or beneath the branches of a lofty forest glade, strangely quickened and stirred by the mysterious play of half-lights, has always spoken eloquently to the soul,

1. From an article by Otto Fischer on Chinese landscape painting in *Das Kunstblatt* (January 1920).

and the builders of temples, mosques, and churches have made full use of it.

Silence is what corresponds to this in the language of musical sounds. 'Yahweh is in his holy temple: let all the earth keep silence before him.' (Hab. ii. 20.) Neither we nor (probably) the prophet any longer bear in mind that this 'keeping silence' (as εὐφημεῖν in Greek), if regarded from the historical, 'genetic' standpoint, springs from the fear of using words of evil omen, which therefore prefers to be altogether speechless. It is the same with Tersteegen in his 'God is present, let all in us be silent'. With prophet and psalmist and poet we feel the necessity of silence from another and quite independent motive. It is a spontaneous reaction to the feeling of the actual *numen praesens*. Once again, what is found coming upon the scene at a higher level of evolution cannot be explained by merely interpolating links in a 'historico-genetic' chain of development; and the Psalmist and Tersteegen and even we ourselves are at least as interesting subjects for the analysis of the psychologist of religion as are the 'primitives', with their habitual practice of εὐφημία, the silence that merely avoids words of ill augury.

Besides silence and darkness Oriental art knows a third direct means for producing a strongly numinous impression, to wit, *emptiness* and *empty distances*. Empty distance, remote vacancy, is, as it were, the sublime in the horizontal. The wide-stretching desert, the boundless uniformity of the steppe, have real sublimity, and even in us Westerners they set vibrating chords of the numinous along with the note of the sublime, according to the principle of the association of feelings. Chinese architecture, which is essentially an art in the laying out and grouping of buildings, makes a wise and very striking use of this fact. It does not achieve the impression of solemnity by lofty vaulted halls or imposing altitudes, but nothing could well be more solemn than the silent amplitude of the enclosed spaces, courtyards, and vestibules which it employs. The imperial tombs of the Ming emperors at Nanking and Peking are, perhaps, the strongest example of this, including, as they do, in their plan the empty distances of an entire landscape. Still more interesting is the part played by the factor of void or emptiness in Chinese painting. There it has almost become a special art to paint empty space, to make it palpable, and to develop variations upon this singular theme. Not only are there pictures upon which 'almost nothing' is painted, not only is it an essential feature of their style to make the strongest impression with the fewest strokes and the scantiest means, but there are very many pictures – especially such as are connected with contemplation – which impress the observer with the feeling that the void itself is depicted as a subject, is indeed the main subject of the picture. We can only understand this by recalling what was said above on the 'nothingness' and the 'void' of the mystics and on the enchantment and spell exercised by the 'negative hymns'. For 'void' is, like darkness and silence, a negation, but a negation that does away with every 'this' and 'here', in order that the 'wholly other' may become actual.

Not even music, which else can give manifold expression to all the feelings of the mind, has any positive way to express 'the holy'. Even the most consummate Mass-music can only give utterance to the holiest, most numinous moment in the Mass – the moment of transubstantiation – by sinking into stillness: no mere momentary pause, but an absolute cessation of sound long enough for us to 'hear the silence' itself; and no devotional moment in the whole Mass approximates in impressiveness to this 'keeping silence before the Lord'. It is instructive to submit Bach's Mass in B minor to the test in this matter. Its most mystical portion is the 'Incarnatus' in the 'Credo', and there the effect is due to the faint, whispering, lingering sequence in the fugue structure, dying away *pianissimo*. The held breath and hushed sound of the passage, its weird cadences, sinking away in lessened thirds, its pauses and syncopations, and its rise and fall in astonishing semitones, which render so well the sense of awe-struck wonder – all this serves to express the *mysterium* by way of intimation, rather than in forthright utterance. And by this means Bach attains his aim here far better than in the 'Sanctus'. This latter is, indeed, an incomparably successful expression of Him, whose is 'the power and the glory', an enraptured and triumphant choric hymn to perfect and absolute sovereignty. But it is very far distant from the mood of the text that accompanies the music, which is taken from Isa. vi, and which the composer should have interpreted in accordance with that passage as a whole. No one would gather from this magnificent chorus that the Seraphim covered their faces with two of their wings.[1] In this point Mendelssohn shows very fine sensibility in his musical setting of Ps. ii at the words (v. 11): 'Serve the Lord with fear, and rejoice with trembling.' And here too the matter is expressed less in the music itself than in the way the music is restrained and repressed – one might almost say, abashed – as the Cathedral choir at Berlin so well knows how to render it. And, if a final example may be cited, the 'Popule meus' of Thomas Luiz gets as near to the heart of the matter as any music can. In this the first chorus sings the first words of the *Trisagion*: 'Hagios, ho theos, hagios ischyros, hagios athanatos', and the second chorus sings in response the Latin rendering of the words: 'Sanctus deus, sanctus fortis, sanctus immortalis', each chorus thrilling with a sort of muffled tremor. But the *Trisagion* itself, sung *pianissimo* by singers kept out of sight far at the back, is like a whisper floating down through space, and is assuredly a consummate reproduction of the scene in the vision of Isaiah.

1. The Jewish tradition has been, however, very well aware of the import of the matter. In the splendid New Year's Day Hymn of Melek Elyōn the words run: 'All the mighty ones on high *whisper low*: Yahweh is King.'

The Numinous in the Old Testament

WHILE the feelings of the non-rational and numinous constitute a vital factor in every form religion may take, they are pre-eminently in evidence in Semitic religion and most of all in the religion of the Bible. Here mystery lives and moves in all its potency. It is present in the ideas of the daemonic and angelic world, which, as a 'wholly other', surrounds, transcends, and permeates this world of ours; it is potent in the Biblical eschatology and the ideal of a 'kingdom of God' contrasted with the natural order, now as being future in time, now as being eternal, but always as the downright marvellous and 'other'; and finally it impresses itself on the character of Yahweh and Elohim – that God who is nevertheless the 'Heavenly Father' of Jesus and as such fulfils, not loses, His character as Yahweh.

The lower stage of numinous consciousness, viz. daemonic dread, has already been long superseded by the time we reach the Prophets and Psalmists. But there are not wanting occasional echoes of it, found especially in the earlier narrative literature. The story in Exod. iv. 24, of how Yahweh in his ὀργή met Moses by the way 'and sought to kill him', still bears this 'daemonic' character strongly, and the tale leaves us almost with the suggestion of a ghostly apparition. And from the standpoint of the more highly developed 'fear of God' one might easily get from this and similar stories the impression that this is not yet religion at all, but a sort of pre-religious, vulgar fear of demons or the like. That would, however, be a misconception; a 'vulgar fear of demons' would refer to a 'demon' in the narrower sense of the word, in which it is a synonym for devil, fiend, or goblin, and is *contrasted* with the divine. But 'demon' in this sense has not been, any more than 'ghost' or 'spectre', a point in the transition, or, if it be preferred, a link in the chain of development which religious consciousness has undergone. Both 'demon' (= fiend) and 'spectre' are, so to speak, offshoots from the true line of progress, spurious fabrications of the fancy accompanying the numinous feeling. We must carefully distinguish from such a 'demon' the δαίμων or 'daemon' in the more general sense of the word, which, if it is not yet itself a 'god', is still less an anti-god, but must be termed a 'pre-god', the numen at a lower stage, in which it is still trammelled and suppressed, but out of which the 'god' gradually grows to more and more lofty manifestations. *This* is the phase whose after-effects can be detected in these ancient stories.

It will be worth while to consider this matter further. Two things may help to an understanding of the real relation with which we are here concerned. First, we may refer back to what was said on an earlier page upon the capacity of 'the dreadful' and 'terrible' in general to attract and arouse, and also to express, the true numinous consciousness or emotion. In the second place, we may refer to the parallel case of music. A man with a pronounced musical faculty, so long as he is a mere raw tyro, may be enraptured by the sound of the bagpipes or the hurdy-gurdy, though perhaps both become intolerable to him when his musical education has been completed. But, if he then recalls the qualitative character of his earlier musical experience and compares it with his present one, he will have to admit that, in both, one and the same side of his mind is functioning, and that what has taken place in the rise of his feeling for music to a more elevated form is no transition to something different in kind, but a process which we may call 'development' or 'growth to maturity', but can hardly further specify. Were we to hear to-day the music of Confucius, it would probably be to us merely a succession of queer noises. Yet already Confucius speaks of the power of music on the mind in a way we moderns cannot better, and touches upon just those elements which we also must recognize in the experience of music. But the most striking consideration in this regard is the way in which some savage tribes are endowed with a capacity for a ready appreciation of our music, which they grasp quickly, practise assiduously, and enjoy intensely, when it is brought before them. This endowment did not first enter their minds at the moment they heard the music by a 'heterogony', 'epigenesis', or other miracle; it simply existed all the time as a natural predisposition or latent capacity. It was aroused and began to develop as soon as the proper incitement came to stimulate it, but to the end it was yet *the selfsame* disposition that had been formerly excited to such primitive and crude manifestations. This 'crude', 'primitive' form of music is often almost or wholly unrecognizable as real music by our developed musical taste, although it was the manifestation of the same impulse and the same element of our psychical nature. Now it is exactly a parallel case when the 'God-fearing' man of to-day finds it hard to detect in the narrative of Exod. iv that which is akin to his own religious experience, or misjudges it altogether. All this involves a point of view which should be taken into consideration more generally with respect to the religion of 'primitive man', though naturally great caution should be used in applying it, seeing that very mistaken conclusions can be drawn from it and there is a real danger of confounding the lower with the higher levels of development and of making too little of the interval between them. However, it is still more dangerous to exclude this point of view altogether, as is unfortunately very commonly done.[1]

Recent research has sought to discover a difference in character between Yahweh, the austere and stern, and Elohim, the familiar, patriarchal God, and there is something very illuminating in the suggestion. Söderblom's supposition[2] is that the notion of Yahweh had its point of origin in earlier 'animistic' ideas. I do not dispute the importance of such 'animistic' ideas in the religious evolutionary process; in fact, I should go even farther than Söderblom in that respect, for he would explain them as a sort of primitive 'philosophy', and therefore has to exclude them altogether from the domain of genuinely *religious* imagination. It would be perfectly compatible with my own view to hold that where ideas of an animistic character had

1. In this regard Mr Marett in particular has important and novel considerations to offer.
2. Söderblom. *Das Werden des Gottesglaubens*, 1916, pp. 297 ff.

been framed they could serve as an important link in the 'chain of stimulation' by which true numinous consciousness is aroused (namely, in so far as they served to disengage and free the obscure feeling-element of 'existent being', latent in it). But what distinguishes Yahweh from El-Shaddai–Elohim is not that the former is an 'anima', but (and the distinction may be applied to differentiate all god-types) that, whereas in Yahweh the numinous preponderates over the familiar 'rational' character, in Elohim the rational aspect outweighs the numinous. 'Outweighs' is as much as we can say, for in Elohim too the numinous element is certainly present; Elohim is, for instance, the subject of the genuinely numinous narrative of the theophany in the burning bush, with the characteristic verse (Exod. iii. 6): 'And Moses hid his face; for he was afraid to look upon God.'

For the copious and diverse characteristics of the idea of God of the ancient Israelites which might be instanced here the reader is referred to works upon the history of religion.[1] The venerable religion of Moses marks the beginning of a process which from that point onward proceeds with ever-increasing momentum, by which the numinous is throughout rationalized and moralized, i.e. charged with ethical import, until it becomes the 'holy' in the fullest sense of the word. The culmination of the process is found in the Prophets and in the Gospels. And it is in this that the special nobility of the religion revealed to us by the Bible is to be found, which, when the stage represented by the 'deutero-Isaiah' is reached, justifies its claim to be a universal world-religion. Here is to be found its manifest superiority over, e.g., Islam, in which Allah is mere 'numen', and is in fact precisely Yahweh in His pre-Mosaic form and upon a larger scale. But this moralizing and rationalizing process does not mean that the numinous itself has been overcome, but merely that its preponderance has been overcome. The numinous is at once the basis upon which and the setting within which the ethical and rational meaning is consummated.

The capital instance of the intimate mutual interpenetration of the numinous with the rational and moral is Isaiah. The note

1. They are given exhaustively in the Encyclopedia *Die Religion in Geschichte und Gegenwart*, vol. ii, pp. 1530, 2036.

struck in the vision of his call is the keynote of his entire prophecy. And nothing is in this regard more significant than the fact that it is in Isaiah that the expression 'the Holy One of Israel' first becomes established as the expression, *par excellence*, for the deity, prevailing over all others by its mysterious potency. This remains so in the writings of the 'deutero-Isaiah', who follows the tradition of the earlier Isaiah. Assuredly in deutero-Isaiah, if in any writer, we have to do with a God whose attributes are clear to conceptual thought: omnipotence, goodness, wisdom, truth; and yet all the time these are attributes of 'the Holy One', whose strange name deutero-Isaiah too repeats no less than fifteen times and always in passages where it has a special impressiveness.

Related expressions akin to the 'holiness' of Yahweh are His 'fury', His 'jealousy', His 'wrath', the 'consuming fire', and the like. The import of them all is not only the all-requiting righteousness of God, not even merely His susceptibility to strong and living emotions, but all this ever enclosed in and permeated with the 'awefulness' and the 'majesty', the 'mystery' and the 'augustness', of His non-rational divine nature.

And this holds good, also, of the expression 'the living God'. God's 'livingness' is perceptibly akin to His 'jealousy' and is manifested in and through this, as in His other 'passions' generally.[1] It is by His 'life' that this God is differentiated from

---

1. Cf. Deut. v. 26: 'For who is there of all flesh, that hath heard the voice of the *living* God speaking out of the midst of the fire, as we have, *and lived*?' Cf. also Josh. iii. 10; 1 Sam. xvii. 26, 36; 2 Kings xix. 4; Isa. xxxvii. 4, 17; Jer. x. 10: 'He is the *living* God, . . . at His *wrath* the earth shall tremble, and the nations shall not be able to abide His *indignation*'; Jer. xxiii. 36; 2 Macc. vii. 33; Matt. xxvi. 63 (the adjuration 'by the *living* God', the God of terror and dread); and Heb. x. 31: 'It is a fearful thing to fall into the hands of the *living* God.' The Old Testament idea of the terrible 'living' God reaches its completion in the ideas of the 'avenging God', of which the most ruthless expression is in the almost appalling image of the treader of the wine-press, Isa. lxiii 3: 'I will tread them in mine anger, and trample them in my fury; and their blood shall be sprinkled upon my garments, and I will stain all my raiment.' The dreadful image recurs in the New Testament in Rev. xix. 15: 'He treadeth the winepress of the fierceness and wrath of Almighty God.'

all mere 'world reason', and becomes this ultimately non-rational essence, that eludes all philosophic treatment. This is the God that lives in the consciousness of all prophets and apostles of the Old and the New Dispensation alike. And all those who later championed against the 'God of philosophy' the 'living God' and the God of anger and love and the emotions have unwittingly been defending the non-rational core of the Biblical conception of God from all excessive rationalization. And so far they were right. Where they were wrong and sank into anthropomorphism was in defending, not figurative 'anger' and 'emotion', but literal anger and emotion, misconceiving the numinous character of the attributes in question and holding them simply to be 'natural' attributes, taken absolutely, instead of realizing that they can only be admitted as figurative indications of something essentially non-rational by means of symbols drawn from feelings that have analogy to it.

We find the power of the numinous – in its phase of the mysterious – to excite and intensify the imagination displayed with particular vividness in Ezekiel. Here are to be classed Ezekiel's dreams and parables and fanciful delineation of God's being and sovereign state, which are, as it were, an example by anticipation of the later more spurious sort of excitement of the religious impulse to the mysterious, leading (in accordance with analogies already expounded) to the merely strange, the extraordinary, the marvellous, and the fantastic. When such an operation of the religious consciousness works itself out in accordance with a wrong analogy, the way is prepared for miracle and legend and the whole dream-world of pseudomysticism; and, though these are all truly enough emanations from the genuine religious experience, they are emanations broken by the opaque, dull medium through which they pass, a mere substitute for the genuine thing, and they end in a vulgar rankness of growth that overspreads the pure feeling of the *mysterium* as it really is and chokes its direct and forthright emotional expression.

But, if Ezekiel hardly shows the numinous moment apart from an admixture of excessive fantasy and imagination, the

same is not true of the Book of Job. In the 38th chapter of Job
we have the element of the mysterious displayed in rare purity
and completeness, and this chapter may well rank among the
most remarkable in the history of religion. Job has been reasoning with his friends against Elohim, and – as far as concerns
them – he has been obviously in the right. They are compelled
to be dumb before him. And then Elohim Himself appears to
conduct His own defence in person. And He conducts it to
such effect that Job avows himself to be overpowered, truly and
rightly overpowered, not merely silenced by superior strength.
Then he confesses: 'Wherefore I abhor myself, and *repent* in
dust and ashes.' That is an admission of inward *convincement*
and conviction, not of impotent collapse and submission to
merely superior power. Nor is there here at all the frame of
mind to which St Paul now and then gives utterance; e.g.
Rom. ix. 20–1: 'Shall the thing formed say to him that formed
it, Why hast thou made me thus? Hath not the potter power
over the clay, of the same lump to make one vessel unto
honour, and another unto dishonour?' To interpret the passage
in Job thus would be a misunderstanding of it. This chapter
does not proclaim, as Paul does, the renunciation of, the realization of the impossibility of, a 'theodicy'; rather, it aims at
putting forward a real theodicy of its own, and a better one
than that of Job's friends; a theodicy able to convict even a Job,
and not only to convict him, but utterly to still every inward
doubt that assailed his soul. For latent in the weird experience
that Job underwent in the revelation of Elohim is at once an
inward relaxing of his soul's anguish and an appeasement, an
appeasement which would alone and in itself perfectly suffice
as the solution of the problem of the Book of Job, even without
Job's rehabilitation in Chapter xlii, where recovered prosperity
comes as an extra payment thrown in after quittance has been
already rendered. But what is this strange 'moment' of experience that here operates at once as a vindication of God to
Job and a reconciliation of Job to God?

In the words put into the mouth of Elohim nearly every note
is sounded which the situation may prepare one to expect *a
priori*: the summons to Job, and the demonstration of God's

overwhelming power, His sublimity and greatness, and His surpassing wisdom. This last would yield forthwith a plausible and rational solution of the whole problem, if only the argument were here completed with some such sentences as: 'My ways are higher than your ways; in my deeds and my actions I have ends that you understand not'; viz. the testing or purification of the godly man, or ends that concern the whole universe as such, into which the single man must fit himself with all his sufferings. If you start from rational ideas and concepts, you absolutely *thirst* for such a conclusion to the discourse. But nothing of the kind follows: nor does the chapter intend at all to suggest such teleological reflections or solutions. In the last resort it relies on something quite different from anything that can be exhaustively rendered in rational concepts, namely, on the sheer absolute wondrousness that transcends thought, on the *mysterium*, presented in its pure, non-rational form. All the glorious examples from nature speak very plainly in this sense. The eagle, that 'dwelleth and abideth on the rock, upon the crag of the rock, and the strong place', whose 'eyes behold afar off' her prey, and whose 'young ones also suck up blood, and where the slain are, there is she' – this eagle is in truth no evidence for the *teleological* wisdom that 'prepares all cunningly and well', but is rather the creature of *strangeness* and *marvel*, in whom the wondrousness of its creator becomes apparent. And the same is true of the ostrich (xxxix. 13–18) with its *inexplicable* instincts. The ostrich is indeed, as here depicted, and 'rationally' considered, a crucial difficulty rather than an evidence of wisdom, and it affords singularly little help if we are seeking *purpose* in nature: 'which leaveth her eggs in the earth, and warmeth them in the dust, and forgetteth that the foot may crush them or that the wild beast may break them. She is hardened against her young ones as though they were not hers: her labour is in vain without fear; because God hath *deprived her of wisdom*, neither hath he imparted to her *understanding*'.

It is the same with the 'wild ass' (verse 5) and the unicorn (verse 9). These are beasts whose complete 'dysteleology' or negation of purposiveness is truly magnificently depicted; but, nevertheless, with their mysterious instincts and their inexplicable behaviour, this very negation of purpose becomes a thing of baffling significance, as in the case of the 'wild goat' (verse 1) and the hind. The 'wisdom' of the inward parts (xxxviii. 36), and the 'knowledge' of dayspring, winds, and clouds, with the mysterious ways in which they come and go, arise and vanish, shift and veer and re-form; and the wonderful Pleiades aloft in heaven, with Orion and 'Arcturus and his sons' – these serve but to emphasize the same lesson. It is conjectured that the descriptions of the hippopotamus (behemoth) and crocodile (leviathan) in xl. 15 ff. are a later interpolation. This may well be the fact; but, if so, it must be admitted that the interpolator has felt the point of the entire section extraordinarily well. He only brings to its grossest expression the thought intended by all the other examples of animals; they gave portents only, he gives us 'monsters' – but 'the monstrous' is just the 'mysterious' in a gross form. Assuredly these beasts would be the most unfortunate examples that one could hit upon if searching for evidences of the purposefulness of the divine 'wisdom'. But they, no less than all the previous examples and the whole context, tenor, and sense of the entire passage, do express in masterly fashion the downright stupendousness, the wellnigh daemonic and wholly incomprehensible character of the eternal creative power; how, incalculable and 'wholly other', it mocks at all conceiving but can yet stir the mind to its depths, fascinate and overbrim the heart. What is meant is the *mysterium* not as mysterious simply, but at the same time also as 'fascinating' and 'august'; and here, too, these latter meanings live, not in any explicit concepts, but in the tone, the enthusiasm, in the very rhythm of the entire exposition. And here is indeed the point of the whole passage, comprising alike the theodicy and the appeasement and calming of Job's soul. The *mysterium*, simply as such, would merely (as discussed above) be a part of the 'absolute inconceivability' of the numen, and that, though it might strike Job utterly dumb, could not convict him inwardly. That of which we are conscious is rather an *intrinsic value* in the incomprehensible – a value inexpressible, positive, and 'fascinating'. This is incommensurable with thoughts of rational human teleology and is not assimilated to them: it remains in all its mystery. But it is as it becomes felt in consciousness that Elohim is justified and at the same time Job's soul brought to peace.

*

A very real parallel to this experience of Job is to be found in the work of a writer of our own day, which is not the less deeply impressive because it is found in the fictitious context of a novel. Max Eyth recounts in his story 'Berufs-Tragik' (in the collection *Hinter Pflug und Schraubstock*) the building of the mighty bridge over the estuary of the Ennobucht. The most profound and thorough labour of the intellect, the most assiduous and devoted professional toil, had gone to the construction of the great edifice, making it in all its significance and purposefulness a marvel of human achievement. In spite of endless difficulties and gigantic obstacles, the bridge is at length finished, and stands defying wind and waves. Then there comes a raging cyclone, and building and builder are swept into the deep. Utter meaninglessness seems to triumph over richest significance, blind 'destiny' seems to stride on its way over prostrate virtue and merit. The narrator tells how he visits the scene of the tragedy and returns again.

When we got to the end of the bridge, there was hardly a breath of wind; high above, the sky showed blue-green, and with an eerie brightness. Behind us, like a great open grave, lay the Ennobucht. The Lord of life and death hovered over the waters in silent majesty. We felt His presence, as one feels one's own hand. And the old man and I knelt down before the open grave and before Him.

Why did they kneel? Why did they feel constrained to do so? One does not kneel before a cyclone or the blind forces of nature, nor even before Omnipotence merely as such. But one does kneel before the wholly uncomprehended Mystery, revealed yet unrevealed, and one's soul is stilled by feeling the way of its working, and therein its justification.

It would be possible to cite many other traces of numinous feeling in the Old Testament. But they have already been admirably put together by one who wrote sixteen hundred years ago in the same sense as we 'upon the non-rational'. This was Chrysostom.[1]

1. See his third discourse, *Περὶ Ἀκαταλήπτου*.

The Numinous in the New Testament

IN the Gospel of Jesus we see the consummation of that process tending to rationalize, moralize, and humanize the idea of God, which began with the earliest period of the old Hebrew tradition and became specially prominent as a living factor in the Prophets and the Psalms, continually bringing the apprehension of the numinous to a richer fulfilment by recognizing in it attributes of clear and profound value for the reason. The result was the faith in 'the fatherhood of God' in that unsurpassable form in which it is peculiar to Christianity.

But in this case, too, it would be a mistake to think that such a rationalization means that 'the numinous' is excluded or superseded. That is a misunderstanding into which we are led by the all-too-plausible delineations of 'Jesus's faith in the fatherhood of God' now prevalent, but it certainly misrepresents the attitude of the first Christian congregations. The error is only possible if we disregard in the message of Christ that which it really purports to be, first, last, and all the time, viz. 'the gospel *of the kingdom*'. As against all rationalizing attempts to tone it down into something less startling, the most recent research shows quite decisively that the 'kingdom' is just greatness and marvel absolute, the 'wholly other' 'heavenly' thing, set in contrast to the world of here and now, 'the mysterious' itself in its dual character as awe-compelling yet all-attracting, glimmering in an atmosphere of genuine 'religious awe'. As such, it sheds a colour, a mood, a tone, upon whatever stands in relation to it, upon the men who proclaim it or prepare for it, upon the life and practice that are its precondition, upon the tidings of it, upon the congregation of those who await it and attain it. All is made into a mystery – all, that is, becomes numinous. This is shown most strikingly in the name by which the company of the disciples call themselves collectively and each other individually, the numinous 'technical term' οἱ ἅγιοι, the holy ones or 'the saints'. It is manifest at once that this does not mean 'the morally perfect' people: it means the people who participate in the mystery of the final Day. Their title is the clear and unambiguous antithesis to the term 'the profane', which we have already met with. For this reason the early Christians are able later to call themselves also actually a 'priestly' – or sacerdotal – 'people', that is, a group of 'consecrated' persons. But the precondition of all this was given with the gospel itself and its claim to be the preaching of the coming kingdom.

What of the Lord of this kingdom, the 'heavenly Father'? As its Lord He is not less, but far more 'holy', 'numinous', mysterious, *qādôsh*, *ἅγιος*, *sacer*, and *sanctus* than His kingdom. He is all these in an absolute degree, and in this aspect of His nature He represents the sublimation and the consummation of all that the old covenant had grasped by way of 'creature-consciousness', 'holy awe', and the like. Not to realize this is to turn the gospel of Jesus into a mere idyll. That these moments do not occur severally in Jesus' message in the form of special 'doctrines' is due to the circumstances already mentioned more than once. But apart from the inherent impossibility of *teaching* them, how could He have had need of 'teaching' what was simply the primary, self-evident fact to every Jew, and especially to every believer in 'the kingdom', namely, that God was 'the Holy One of Israel'? Christ had rather to teach and to proclaim what was *not* self-evident to the Jews, but His own original discovery and revelation, that this very 'Holy One' is a 'heavenly Father'. This point of view necessarily occupied the whole of His 'teaching', and all the more so because it was the point of view thrust sharply into the foreground by the two opposed influences of His time, against both of which the Gospel came historically as a reaction. On the one hand was Pharisaism, with its servitude to Law; on the other, John the Baptist, with his harsh, ascetic interpretation of God; and, in contrast to both, the gospel of the sonhood of man and the fatherhood of God came as the easy yoke, the light burden. But though it is necessarily this new message that the parables and discourses and pronouncements of Jesus complete and fill out, it is in such a way that it always remains an overwhelming and daring paradox, claiming our utmost homage, that He who is 'in heaven' is yet 'our Father'. That that 'heavenly' Being of marvel and mystery and awe is Himself the eternal, benignant, gracious will: this is the resolved contrast that first brings out the deep-felt harmony in true Christian experience; and the harmony cannot be heard aright by the man whose ear does not detect always sounding in it this sublimated 'seventh'.

It is significant, and yet again so natural, that the first petition in the prayer of the Christian fellowship is: 'Hallowed be Thy name.' What I have already said should make the meaning of this clear in its connexion with the Biblical meaning of the word. And we can sometimes detect, even in the teaching of Jesus, notes still vibrating which seem to suggest a trace of that weird awe and shuddering dread before the mysteries of the transcendent of which we have already spoken. Such a passage is Matt. x. 28: 'But rather fear him which is able to *destroy both soul and body in hell.*'

The dark and awful ring of this saying cannot be missed, and it is a rationalization of it merely to refer it to the Judge and His judgement on the Last Day. The same note rings out again clearly in the saying in Heb. x. 31: 'It is a fearful thing to fall into the hands of the living God'; and in Heb. xii. 29: 'Our God is a consuming fire.' (Here the adaptation of Deut. iv. 24: 'The Lord thy God is a consuming fire' into 'Our God is a consuming fire' gives a contrast whose effect enhances the horror of the saying.) And when occasion demands it the Old Testament God of 'vengeance' recurs even in the teaching of Jesus Himself, unveiled and in His own authentic character; as, for instance, in Matt. xxi. 41: 'He will miserably destroy those wicked men.'

Finally, it is in the light of, and with the background of, this numinous experience, with its mystery and its awe – its *mysterium tremendum* – that Christ's Agony in the night of Gethsemane must be viewed, if we are to comprehend or realize at all in our own experience what the import of that agony was. What is the cause of this 'sore amazement' and 'heaviness', this soul shaken to its depths, 'exceeding sorrowful even unto death', and this sweat that falls to the ground like great drops of blood? Can it be ordinary fear of death in the case of one who had had death before his eyes for weeks past and who had just celebrated with clear intent his death-feast with his disciples? No, there is more here than the fear of death; there is the awe of the creature before the *mysterium tremendum*, before the shuddering secret of the numen. And the old tales come back into our mind as strangely parallel and, as it were, prophetically significant, the tales of Yahweh who waylaid Moses by night, and of Jacob who wrestled with God 'until the breaking of the day'. 'He had power with God . . . and prevailed', with the God of 'wrath' and 'fury', with the *numen*, which yet is itself '*my Father*'. In truth even those who cannot recognize 'the Holy One of Israel' elsewhere in the God of the Gospel must at least discover Him here, if they have eyes to see at all.

I have no need to dwell upon the numinous atmosphere pervading the writings of St Paul. 'God dwelleth in a light that none may come nigh.' The 'over-aboundingness' ('exuberance') of the idea of God and the feeling of God leads with Paul to the special terminology and experiences of mysticism.[1] But it is not confined to these: it can be seen alive through all his utterances in the feelings of exalted enthusiasm and his spiritual terminology of the *pneuma*, which are alike far removed from the merely rational side of Christian piety. His dualistic depreciation of 'the flesh', as of all that pertains to creaturehood, is that numinous self-disvaluation spoken of on pp. 65 ff. carried to its extreme. These catastrophes and sudden reversals that befall the religious consciousness, the tragedy of sin and guilt, or again the glow of beatific joy, are only possible and intelligible on the basis of numinous experience. And just as the ὀργὴ θεοῦ with St Paul is more than the mere reaction of

1. As a provisional definition of mysticism I would suggest that, while sharing the nature of religion, it shows a preponderance of its non-rational elements and an over-stressing of them in respect to the 'over-abounding' aspect of the 'numen'. A type of religious experience acquires 'mystical colouring' if it shows an inclination to mysticism. In this sense Christianity since St Paul and St John is not mysticism, but religion with a mystical colouring. And this is justified.

righteous retribution, just as it is permeated by the 'awefulness' of the numinous, so on the other side is the 'fascination' of the experienced love of God, that bears the spirit beyond its boundaries into the third heaven, more than the mere consummation of the natural human feeling of a child for its parent. The ὀργὴ θεοῦ is potently and vividly present in the grand passage in Rom. i. 18 ff., where we recognize directly the jealous, passionate Yahweh of the Old Testament, here grown to a God of the Universe of fearful power, who pours out the blazing vials of His wrath over the whole world. In this passage there is an intuition, genuinely non-rational in character, the sublimity of which has an almost horrible quality: that the commission of sin is the angry God's punishment for sin. St Paul reiterates this thought – so intolerable, if considered 'rationally' – in three separate verses. 'Wherefore God also gave them up to uncleanness through the lusts of their own hearts, to dishonour their own bodies between themselves' (Rom. i. 24); 'For this cause God gave them up unto vile affections' (i. 26); 'God gave them over to a reprobate mind, . . . being filled with all unrighteousness', etc. (i. 28, 29).

To feel the full weight and force of this intuition it is necessary to escape as far as possible from the mental atmosphere of our dogmatic interpretations and judiciously toned-down catechisms, and to try to recapture the awe that could be felt by the Jew toward the fury of Yahweh, by the Hellenistic Greek toward the horror of *heimarmenē* or Destiny, and by primitive man in general toward the *ira deorum* or anger of the gods.

There is one other point in the teaching of Paul that demands notice in this connexion – his doctrine of predestination. It is perhaps precisely the 'rationalist' who feels most directly that with the idea of predestination we are standing on downright non-rational ground. Nothing remains so alien to the rationalist as this doctrine. And from his point of view he is quite right; from the standpoint of the rational this notion of predestination is a sheer absurdity, an absolute offence. Let him acquiesce in all the paradoxes of the Trinity and Christology, predestination will yet remain perpetually to confront him as a stumbling-block.

Not, as need hardly be said, in the form in which it has been put forward since the time of Schleiermacher, following the tradition of Leibniz and Spinoza. That is simply a capitulation to natural law and *causae secundae*, a surrender to the claim of modern psychology that all human resolves and actions are subject to the compelling force of motives, so that a man is unfree and predetermined thereby. And so, this predetermination by *nature*, having been identified with the all-embracing efficacy of God, in the end the outcome of the profound and purely religious intuition of divine predetermination – which has no concern at all with 'laws of nature' – is the comparatively trivial 'scientific' notion of universal causal connexion. There can be no more spurious product of theological speculation, no more fundamental falsification of religious conceptions than this; and it is certainly not against this that the rationalist feels an antagonism, for it is itself a piece of solid rationalism, but at the same time a complete abandonment of the real religious idea of 'predestination'.

This false 'scientific' interpretation of 'predestination' having been put aside, it may be shown that as a religious idea it springs from two sources and has two quite distinct aspects, which should be distinguished by separate names. The one is 'election', the other – striking an essentially different note – 'predestination' proper.

The idea of 'election' – i.e. of having been chosen out and pre-ordained by God *unto salvation* – is an immediate and pure expression of the actual religious experience of grace. The recipient of divine grace feels and knows ever more and more surely, as he looks back on his past, that he has not grown into his present self through any achievement or effort of his own, and that, apart from his own will or power, grace was imparted to him, grasped him, impelled and led him. And even the resolves and decisions that were most his own and most free become to him, without losing the element of freedom, something that he *experienced* rather than *did*. Before every deed of his own he sees love the deliverer in action, seeking and selecting, and acknowledges that an eternal gracious purpose is watching over his life. But this 'pre-ordainment' is purely a pre-ordainment unto salvation and has in itself nothing to do with the *praedestinatio ambigua*, the predetermination of all men *either* to be saved *or* to be damned. The rational and logical conclusion of course would be that, if he is elected of God but others are not, God, in appointing the elect to bliss, determines also the rejected for damnation. But this conclusion is not, and must not be, drawn, for what we are concerned with is a religious intuition which, as such, stands alone and is only warrant for itself, and which indeed is outraged by any attempt to weave it into a system or make it yield a series of inferences. In this respect Schleiermacher is quite right when he says in his *Discourses upon Religion*:[1] 'Every (*sc.* religious) intuition is a self-subsistent work ... knowing nothing of derivation and point of connexion.'

So much for 'election'. From it must be distinguished 'predestination' proper, as it appears in St Paul, e.g. Rom. i.x 18: 'Therefore hath he mercy on whom he will ... and whom he will he hardeneth.'

It is true that the thought of 'election', prominent in St Paul, can be detected here as well. But the reflection in v. 20 is obviously the utterance of quite a different frame of mind: 'Nay but, O man, who art thou that repliest against God? Shall the thing formed say to him that formed it, Why hast thou made me thus?' That is a line of thought wholly out of keeping with the set of ideas centring about 'election'. And yet even less can it be derived from any abstractly theoretic 'doctrine' of the all-causing nature of God. Such a doctrine we find in Zwingli, and with him it does indeed give rise to a 'doctrine of predestination', but one that is rather the artificial product of philosophical speculation than the result of immediate religious experience. The true 'predestination', springing directly from religious intuition, has its origin beyond question in St Paul. But in him it is easily recognized as the numinous feeling in face of the *mysterium tremendum*; and that unique phase of it that we met with above

1. Schleiermacher, *Reden über die Religion*, ed. R. Otto, 4th ed., pp. 37–8.

(pp. 23 ff.) in the narrative of Abraham recurs here in a signally intensified form. For the religious conception in the notion of predestination is nothing but that 'creature-consciousness', that self-abasement and the annulment of personal strength and claims and achievements in the presence of the transcendent, as such. The numen, overpoweringly experienced, becomes the all-in-all. The creature, with his being and doing, his 'willing' and 'running' (Rom. ix. 16), his schemes and resolves, becomes nothing. The conceptual expression to indicate such a felt submergence and annihilation over against the numen is then – here impotence and there omnipotence; here the futility of one's own choice, there the will that ordains all and determines all.

It is next to be noted that 'predestination' in this sense, as identical with the absolute supremacy of the numen, has nothing whatever to do with the 'unfree will' of 'Determinism'. Rather, it finds very frequently precisely in the 'free will' of the creature the contrast which makes it stand out so prominently. 'Will what thou wilt and how thou canst; plan and choose; yet must all come about as it shall and as is determined': that is the earliest and most genuine expression of the matter. In face of the eternal power man is reduced to naught, *together with* his free choice and action. And the eternal power waxes immeasurable just because it fulfils its decrees *despite* the freedom of human will. This is the aspect of the matter designedly thrust into the foreground in many typical Mohammedan narratives which profess to display the inflexibility of the decrees of Allah. In these, men are *able* to devise and decide and reject; but, however they choose or act, Allah's eternal will is accomplished to the very day and hour that was ordained. The purport of this is precisely, *not* that God and God alone is an active cause, but rather that the activity of the creature, be it never so vigorous and free, is overborne and determined absolutely by the eternal operative purpose.[1] The thought of the deity as the absolutely sole

1. The story told by Beidhavi, an expositor of the Koran, illustrates this: Once when Azrael, the angel of Death, came before Solomon he directed his gaze upon one of the king's companions. 'Who is that?'

and all-embracing active cause first occurs where the creature-feeling is intensified still further, and is at the same time combined with theoretic considerations. It then leads to mysticism; and it is only again a further consequence if the speculations about being, peculiar to and characteristic of mysticism, become then attached to the thought of God as sole cause. To the creature then is denied, not merely *efficacy* as a cause, but true *reality* and complete being, and all existence and fullness of being is ascribed to the absolute entity, who alone really *is*, while all 'being' of creatures is either a function of this absolute Being – which brings them into existence – or mere illusion. This sequence of ideas is found in particularly explicit form in the mysticism of Geulincx and the Occasionalists. 'Ubi nihil vales, ibi nihil velis.' Sometimes we hear the same mystical chord in St Paul also, as in his mysterious saying about the final issue of all things, where 'God shall be all in all'. But the passage in Romans is different. It goes no farther than the thought of predestination itself; and predestination we have found to be nothing but the intensified 'creature-feeling' in conceptual expression, and to be altogether rooted in the numinous consciousness.

A further consideration may make it plainer that this must be so. If it be really true that the consciousness of the numinous, as 'creature-feeling', is the root of the predestination idea, then we should expect that the form of religious faith marked by an undue and exaggerated insistence on the non-rational elements in the idea of God would also lean most markedly to predestination. And such is obviously the case. No religion has such a leaning to predestination as Islam; and

asked the man. 'The angel of death,' replied Solomon. 'He seems to be looking at me,' continued the other, 'so command the wind that it bear me hence and set me down in India.' Solomon did so. Then said the angel, 'I gazed upon him for so long out of astonishment, seeing it had been commanded me to fetch his soul out of India, while he was yet with thee in Canaan.' This is a predestination which presupposes free will just as its foil. However freely man makes his plans, Allah has always set his countermine.

[This story is told in verse by Leigh Hunt in his poem *The Inevitable*; cf. Oxford ed. (1922), pp. 95–6. (*Trans.*)]

the special quality of Islam is just that in it, from its commencement onwards, the rational and specifically moral aspect of the idea of God was unable to acquire the firm and clear impress that it won, e.g., in Christianity or Judaism. In Allah the numinous is absolutely preponderant over everything else. So that, when Islam is criticized for giving a merely 'fortuitous' character to the claim of morality, as though the moral law were only valid through the chance caprice of the deity, the criticism is well justified, only 'chance' and fortuitousness have nothing to do with the matter. The explanation is rather that the numinous in Allah, nay, even his uncanny and daemonic character, outweighs what is rational in him. And this will account for what is commonly called the 'fanatical' character of this religion. Strongly excited feeling of the numen, that runs to frenzy, untempered by the more rational elements of religious experience – that is everywhere the very essence of fanaticism.

The above interpretation of the notion of predestination gives at the same time our estimate of it. It is an attempted statement, in conceptual terms and by *analogy*, of something that at bottom is incapable of explication by concepts. Fully justified in this sense as an analogical expression, it is wholly unjustified (*summum jus* becoming *summa injuria*) if its character as analogy is missed, so that it is taken as an adequate formulation of theological theory. In that case it is disastrous and intolerable to a rational religion like Christianity, in spite of the attempts that are made to render it innocuous by all the arts of evasion and mitigation.

There is another element in the thought of Paul besides his notion of predestination that is rooted in the numinous: I refer to his utter depreciation of 'the flesh'. 'The flesh' with Paul is simply the condition of the creature in general. And this is utterly disparaged and depreciated by the numinous consciousness (as we saw on pp. 23 ff., 65 ff.) in contrast to the transcendent, both in regard to its existence and its value; in respect to the first as 'dust and ashes', 'nothingness', insufficient, weak, transient, and perishing, and in respect to the second as the 'profane', the impure, which is unable to assume the worth of holiness or to come into its presence. We find these two same sorts of depreciation among the ideas of Paul, and the specifically Pauline feature in them is only the vigour and completeness with which he expresses them. It is a quite separate question whence Paul derives this intensity in his denunciation and depreciation of 'the flesh', whether it is original to him or stimulated by the 'dualistic' environment of thought in which he moved. As has been already said, one can determine nothing about the essential nature or the value of a thing by tracing its genesis and continuous historic derivation from other sources. And at least we may maintain that Paul might well be stimulated to this emphatic expression by many genuine cases of the numinous experience recorded in the Old Testament. There too *bāsār*, the flesh, is both the principle of being 'dust and ashes' and the principle of the 'pollution' of the creature in the presence of holiness.

In St John, no less than in St Paul, there is a strong strain of the numinous. The element of 'awefulness', it is true, dies away in him, as so commonly in mysticism, without ever quite vanishing, for, *pace* Ritschl, even in John 'the wrath of God abideth' (John iii. 36); but this only makes the elements of 'mystery' and 'fascination' the stronger, even in their mystical form. In John, Christianity absorbs $\phi\hat{\omega}\varsigma$ and $\zeta\omega\acute{\eta}$, 'light' and 'life', into itself from the religions at rivalry with it;[1] and justly so, for only in Christianity do they win home. But what is this 'light' and this 'life'? Not to *feel* what they are is to be made of wood, but none can express it. They are a sheer abounding overplus of the non-rational element in religion.

1. And thereby drains these religions of their life-blood, according to 'the right of the stronger'. And henceforth these elements belong to Christianity indissolubly as its very own. For

> Wenn starke Geisteskraft
> Die Elemente
> An sich herangerafft:
> Ken Engel trennte
> Geeinte Zwienatur
> Der innigen Beiden –

and still less can the criticism of scholars! ['When the vigour of the spirit has gathered the elements into itself, then may no angel sunder the double nature now made single of the united twain.']

And the same is true even of that saying of St John to which the 'rationalists' are so specially fond of referring: 'God is a Spirit' (John iv. 24). This was the text on account of which Hegel held Christianity to be the highest because the most truly spiritual (*geistig*) religion. But Hegel meant by 'spirit' the 'absolute reason'. St John when he speaks of πνεῦμα is not thinking of 'absolute reason' but of that which is in absolute contrast to everything of 'the world' and 'the flesh', the utterly mysterious and miraculous heavenly Being who surpasses all the understanding and reason of the 'natural' man. He is thinking of that 'Spirit' which 'bloweth where it listeth, and thou hearest the sound thereof, but canst not tell whence it cometh and whither it goeth' – the Spirit which just on that account is not confined to Zion or Gerizim, and whose worship is only for those who are themselves 'in spirit and in truth'. So that this saying, apparently wholly 'rational' in import, is itself the strongest and clearest indication of the non-rational element in the Biblical idea of God.[1]

1. Compare with this chapter my book *Reich Gottes und Menschensohn* (*The Kingdom of God and the Son of Man*).

The Numinous in Luther

In Catholicism the feeling of the numinous is to be found as a living factor of singular power. It is seen in Catholic forms of worship and sacramental symbolism, in the less authentic forms assumed by legend and miracle, in the paradoxes and mysteries of Catholic dogma, in the Platonic and neo-Platonic strands woven into the fabric of its religious conceptions, in the solemnity of churches and ceremonies, and especially in the intimate *rapport* of Catholic piety with mysticism. For reasons already suggested, the mysterious is much less in evidence in the official systems of doctrine, whether Catholic or Protestant. Particularly since the time when the great medieval scholastics (the *theologi moderni*, so called) replaced Plato by Aristotle and welded the latter and his method on to the doctrines of the Church, Catholic orthodoxy has been subjected to a strong rationalizing influence, to which, however, actual living religious practice and feeling never conformed or corresponded. The battle here joined between so-called 'Platonism' and 'Aristotelianism', and in general the long persistent protest against the scholastics, is itself in large part nothing but the struggle between the rational and the non-rational elements in the Christian religion. And the same antithesis is clearly operative as a factor in Luther's protest against Aristotle and the *theologi moderni*.

At that time Plato himself was known (very imperfectly) chiefly through the interpretations – and misinterpretations – of him by Augustine, Plotinus, and Dionysius the Areopagite. Yet it was a true feeling that led the contrasted attitudes of mind to choose the names of Plato and Aristotle as their battle-cries. Plato did indeed make a powerful contribution towards the rationalization of his religion, for according to his *philosophy* the deity had to become identical with the 'Idea of the Good', and consequently something wholly rational and conceivable. But the most remarkable characteristic of Plato's thought is just that he himself finds science and philosophy too narrow to comprise the whole of man's mental life. He has indeed properly no philosophy of religion; he grasps the object of religion by quite different means than those of conceptual thinking, viz. by the 'ideograms' of myth, by 'enthusiasm' or inspiration, 'erôs' or love, 'mania' or the divine frenzy. He abandons the attempt to bring the object of religion into one system of knowledge with the objects of 'science' (ἐπιστήμη), i.e. reason, and it becomes something not less but greater thereby; while at the same time it is just this that allows the sheer non-rational aspect of it to be so vividly felt in Plato, and indeed vividly expressed as well as felt. No one has enunciated more definitively than this master-thinker that God transcends all reason, in the sense that He is beyond the powers of our conceiving, not merely beyond our powers of comprehension.

Therefore is it an *impossible* task both to discover the creator and father of this whole universe and to publish the discovery of him in words for all to understand.[1]

Aristotle's thought is much more theological than Plato's, but his temper is far less religious; and at the same time his theology is absolutely rationalistic. And this contrast between the two is repeated among those who profess themselves 'Platonists' or 'Aristotelians'.

Another influence which orthodox doctrine underwent, from the earliest patristic period onwards, and which tended to weaken the non-rational element in religion, came from

1. *Timaeus*, 28 c τὸν μὲν οὖν ποιητὴν καὶ πατέρα τοῦδε τοῦ παντὸς εὑρεῖν τε ἔργον καὶ εὑρόντα εἰς πάντας ἀδύνατον λέγειν. For the non-rational and supra-rational strain in Plato the reader is referred to von Wilamowitz-Möllendorff, *Plato*, i. 418: and especially to the splendid passage from Plato's seventh letter: 341 c: 'Concerning these things [*sc.* ultimate truth] there is not, nor will there be, any treatise written by me. For they do not at all admit of being expounded in writing, as do objects of other [scientific] studies. . . . Only after long, arduous conversance with the matter itself . . . a light suddenly breaks upon the soul as from a kindled flame, and once born keeps alive of itself. . . . Only to a few men is the exposition of these things of any profit, and they only need a slight indication of them for their discovery.'

the acceptance of the ancient theory of the divine ἀπάθεια or immunity from passion. The God of Greek, and especially of Stoic, theology was constructed after the ideal of the 'wise man', who achieves this 'apathy' by the overcoming of his 'passions' and 'affections'; and the attempt was now made to assimilate this God to the 'living God' of Scripture. And, as intimated above, an effective if unconscious factor in this contest was the antithesis between the non-rational and the rational aspects of the deity. Lactantius, in his treatise *De Ira Dei*, illustrates particularly strikingly this fight against the God of the philosophers. He uses the same wholly rational terms, taken from man's emotional life, as do his opponents, but raises them to a higher power, so that he makes God, as it were, a gigantic mind, quick with an immense vitality. But whoever in this way contends for the 'living God' is at the same time contending unwittingly for the divine in God, that which cannot be reduced to idea, world-order, moral order, principle of being, or purposive will. And many of Lactantius' own expressions point of themselves to something beyond. Thus, quoting Plato, he says: 'Quid omnino sit Deus, non esse quaerendum: quia nec inveniri possit nec enarrari.'[1] He is in general fond of emphasizing the *incomprehensibilitas* of God: 'quem nec aestimare sensu valeat humana mens nec eloqui lingua mortalis. Sublimior enim ac maior est, quam ut possit aut cogitatione hominis aut sermone comprehendi.'[2] He is fond of the expression *maiestas Dei*, and blames the philosophers for misjudging the 'unique majesty' of God. And he feels the *tremendum* in the *maiestas* when he asserts that God 'is wroth', and demands 'awe' as a fundamental characteristic of religion when he says: 'Ita fit, ut religio et maiestas et honor *metu* constet. Metus autem non est, ubi nullus irascitur.'[3] He says that a God who cannot be angry cannot love either: and a God

1. Ed. Fritzsche, p. 227: 'We ought not to ask what God is altogether; for it can neither be discovered by any nor stated in words.'

2. Ibid., p. 116: '[God] whom the human mind has no power to appraise, nor tongue of mortals to utter. For he is too sublime and too great to be grasped in the thought or the speech of man.'

3. 'Thus it comes that religion and majesty and honour depend upon fear. But there is no fear where none is angry.'

that knows neither love nor anger would be *immobilis* and not the 'Deus *vivus*', the *living* God of Scripture.

This ancient battle of Lactantius against the *deus philosophorum* comes to life again in the Middle Ages in Duns Scotus's battle for the God of 'willing', as opposed to the God of 'being', and for the validity of volition as an essential in religion, as opposed to cognition. And the non-rational elements which are still latent in Duns Scotus break out openly in Luther in a whole series of some of his most characteristic thoughts.

This aspect of Luther's religion was later tacitly expunged, and is to-day readily dismissed as 'not the authentic Luther', or as 'a residuum of the scholastic speculations of the nominalists'. But, if that is so, it is strange that this 'residuum of Scholasticism' exercised such a power in Luther's own mental life as it palpably did. In point of fact this is not a 'residuum' at all, but beyond all question the mysterious background of his religious life, obscure and 'uncanny', and to estimate it in all its power and profundity we need to abstract the lucid bliss and joyfulness of Luther's faith in the divine grace, and to see this faith in relation to the background of that mysterious experience on which it rests. It matters not from what source, whether 'nominalism' or the traditional teaching of his Order, his consciousness was first stirred; we have in any case in Luther the numinous consciousness at first hand, stirred and agitated through its typical 'moments', as we have come to know them. It is a corroboration that these 'moments' appear in Luther in their completed series, and so point back to the common basis that unites them all.

1. We are not here concerned with the many strands, strong at the outset, weaker later, but never altogether disappearing, that connect him with mysticism. Nor are we concerned with the surviving effects of the 'numinous' element of the Catholic worship in his doctrine of the Eucharist, which cannot be wholly derived either from his doctrine of the forgiveness of sins or from his deference to the written word of scripture. Let us rather consider Luther's *mirae speculationes*

upon the 'unrevealed' in God in contrast to the *facies Dei revelata* (revealed face of God), upon the *divina maiestas* and the *omnipotentia Dei* in contrast to His *gratia*, as he treats of them in his work *De Servo Arbitrio*. The investigation as to how far Luther took over 'doctrines' from Scotus does not amount to much; they stand in most intimate connexion with his own innermost religious life, of which they are a genuine first-hand utterance, and should be examined as such. Luther himself guarantees expressly that he does not teach such things merely as subjects of dispute in the schools or as philosophical deductions and corollaries, but because they are a central part of the religious experience of the Christian, who must know them in order to have faith and to have life. He rejects the cautious foresight of Erasmus' view, that such things should at least be withheld from the common people, preaching them himself in public sermons (for example, upon Exodus, in reference to the hardening of Pharaoh's heart) and writing them in his letter to the men of Antwerp. And again, just before his death, speaking of his book *De Servo Arbitrio*, in which these ideas stand clearly expressed, Luther acknowledges that nothing he wrote was so truly his own.

Is this borne out in his general teaching? His words in the *Great Catechism*, 'To have a God is nothing else than to trust Him from the heart', might seem to imply the negative. And certainly to Luther God is He who 'overbrims with pure goodness'. Yet this same Luther knows depths and abysses in the Godhead that make his heart despond, from which he flees for refuge to the 'Word', like a 'hare to his cleft in the rocks', flees, it may be, to the Sacrament or to absolution, or to the comforting official pronouncements of Dr Pommeranus, but in general no less to every word of comfort or promise in the Psalms and the Prophets. But that before which his soul quails again and again in awe is not merely the stern Judge, demanding righteousness – for He is wholly a 'God of revelation' – but rather at the same time God in His 'unrevealedness', in the awful majesty of His very Godhead; He before whom trembles not simply the transgressor of the law, but the creature, as such, in his 'uncovered' creaturehood.

Luther even ventures to designate this awe-inspiring, non-rational character of deity as 'Deus ipse, ut est in sua natura et maiestate'[1] (an assumption which would be in fact a dangerous and erroneous one; for no distinction of the non-rational and the rational aspects of God should imply that the latter is less essential than the former).

The passages relevant in this connexion from Luther's *De Servo Arbitrio* are cited often enough: but to understand the wellnigh daemonic character of this numinous feeling the reader should particularly note the effect of the following passage from Luther's sermon on Exod. xx. The preacher leaves no means untried to bring out effectively the element of numinous horror in his text:

> Yea, for the world it seemeth as though God were a mere silly yawner, with mouth ever agape, or a cuckold, who lets another lie with his wife and feigneth that he sees it not.
> But He assaileth a man, and *hath such a delight* therein that He is of His jealousy and wrath impelled to *consume* the wicked.
> Then shall we learn how that God is a consuming fire . . . That is then the consuming, devouring fire. . . . Wilt thou sin? Then will He *devour thee up*. . . . For God is a fire, that consumeth, devoureth, rageth; verily He is your undoing, as fire consumeth a house and maketh it dust and ashes.

And in another place:

> Yea, He is more terrible and frightful than the Devil. For He dealeth with us and bringeth us to ruin with power, smiteth and hammereth us and payeth no heed to us. . . . In His majesty He is a consuming fire. . . . For therefrom can no man refrain: if he thinketh on God aright, his heart in his body is struck with terror. . . . Yea, as soon as he heareth God named, he is filled with trepidation and fear.[2]

It is the absolute numen, felt here partially in its aspect of *maiestas* and *tremendum*. And the reason I introduced these terms above to denote the one side of the numinous experience was in fact just because I recalled Luther's own expressions,

1. 'God Himself, as He is in his own very nature and majesty.'
2. *Vide* the Erlangen edition of Luther's works, xxxvi, pp. 210 ff. 222, 231, 237; xxxv, p. 167; xlvii, p. 145; l, p. 200.

and borrowed them from his *divina maiestas* and *metuenda voluntas*, which have rung in my ears from the time of my earliest study of Luther. Indeed, I grew to understand the numinous and its difference from the rational in Luther's *De Servo Arbitrio* long before I identified it in the *qādôsh* of the Old Testament and in the elements of 'religious awe' in the history of religion in general.

One must have beheld these gulfs and abysses in Luther to understand aright how significant it is that it is the same man who, on the other hand, endeavours to put the whole of Christianity into a confiding faith. The same contrast noted above in the religion of the Gospel and in the paradoxes of the 'faith in God the Father', recurs in the religious experience of Luther, but in unexampled intensity. That it is the *un-approachable* which becomes approachable, the *Holy One* who is pure goodness, that it is *'Majesty'* which makes itself familiar and intimate – there is the inwardness of the matter, and this finds only very dubious expression in the subsequent one-sided doctrine of the schools, where the mystical character of the 'wrath' – which is of the essence of 'holiness' infused with that of 'goodness' – is referred simply to the righteousness of God, and taken thus as righteous anger or indignation.

2. Once the numinous consciousness has been aroused, it is to be expected, seeing that it is a unity, that one of its 'moments' will be found to be bound up with the rest. In the case of Luther we find next after this element of 'wrath' the numinous manifesting itself in the set of ideas which we may fairly call those of Job. The Book of Job, as was seen above, is not so much concerned with the *awefulness* of the majesty of the numen as with its *mysteriousness*; it is concerned with the non-rational in the sense of the irrational, with sheer paradox baffling comprehension, with that which challenges the 'reasonable' and what might be reasonably expected, which goes directly against the grain of reason. To this place belong Luther's violent onslaughts upon the 'whore Reason', which must seem grotesque to anyone who has not rightly grasped the problem of the non-rational element in the idea of God. But certain set phrases, constantly recurring in Luther

and very typical of him, are specially significant in this
connexion, as showing the strong feeling he had for the non-
rational aspect of the divine nature in general. The most
interesting passages are not those in which he gives this
feeling currency in the small change of popular edification,
that soothes itself with the thought that God's ways are too
high for us men; but those in which he lays hold of some
startling paradox. He can indeed tell in quite a homely and
popular way 'how strange a lord our God is', and refer this
to the fact that God does not esteem or count as the world
counts, and that He disciplines us by the strange ways of His
guidance. Such expressions are of general currency; but
others – and these the more characteristic – strike a loftier
note. God is altogether 'mysteriis suis et iudiciis impervesti-
gabilis' ('beyond tracking out in His mysteries and His
judgements'), displays – as in Job – His 'vera maiestas' 'in
metuendis mirabilibus et iudiciis suis incomprehensibilibus'
('in His fearful marvels and incomprehensible judgements'),
is in His essence hidden away from all reason, knows no
measure, law, or aim, and is verified in the paradox: 'ut
ergo fidei locus sit, opus est, ut omnia, quae creduntur,
abscondantur' ('in order, therefore, that there may be a place
for faith, all the things that are believed must be hidden away').
And his concern is not simply to note this as an inconceivable
paradox, to acknowledge it and bow before it, but to recognize
that such a paradox is essential to the nature of God and even
its distinguishing characteristic.

Si enim talis esset eius iustitia, quae humano captu posset
iudicari esse iusta, *plane non esset divina* et nihilo differret ab
humana iustitia. At cum sit Deus verus et unus, deinde totus
incomprehensibilis et inaccessibilis humana ratione, par est,
immo necessarium est, ut et iustitia sua sit incomprehensibilis.[1]

1. 'For were His justice such as could be adjudged as just by
the human understanding it were manifestly not divine, and would
differ in nothing from human justice. But since God is true and single,
yea in His entirety incomprehensible and inaccessible to human
reason, it is right, nay it follows necessarily, that His justice also is
incomprehensible.'

Theology gives expression to its perplexed endeavour to find a name for the elements of the non-rational and the mysterious in the repulsive doctrine that God is *exlex* (outside the law), that good is good because God wills it, instead of that God wills it because it is good, a doctrine that results in attributing to God an absolutely fortuitous will, which would in fact turn Him into a 'capricious despot'. These doctrines are specially prominent in the theology of Islam, and this can be immediately understood if the two positions we maintain are sound, viz. that such doctrines are really perplexed expressions of the non-rational, numinous side of the divine nature, and that this is altogether the preponderant aspect in Islam. And we find them also in Luther in the same connexion. In this very fact, however, lies the excuse for doctrines in themselves so blasphemous and horrible: they are caricatures prompted by a deficient psychology and a mistaken choice of expressions, and not by any disregard of the absoluteness of moral values.

3. From the point of view already considered in detail it will be seen that, with such feelings as a basis, it was inevitable that the doctrine of predestination would in due course make its appearance in Luther's religion. And in his case we do not need, as we did in the case of Paul, to *postulate* the close inner connexion between this doctrine and the numinous temper, for in the *De Servo Arbitrio* it is palpably evident. The one explicitly depends upon the other, and the inward bond of union between the two is so unmistakable that this treatise of Luther's becomes a sort of psychological key to related phases of religious experience.

It is only occasionally that these purely numinous elements in Luther's religious consciousness are displayed so strongly and forcibly as in the treatise *De Servo Arbitrio*. But in his battles with '*desperatio*' and with Satan, in his constantly recurring religious catastrophes and fits of melancholy, in his wrestlings for grace, perpetually renewed, which bring him to the verge of mental disorder, in all these there are more than merely rational elements at work in his soul. Moreover, even when he is speaking solely in rational terms of judgement, punishment, and the wrath of God, we must, if we are to recapture the real Luther in these expressions, hear sounding in them the profoundly non-rational strain of 'religious awe'. For this wrath of God also has often, perhaps has always, something in it of that fury of Yahweh, that ὀργή of the numen.

4. This circumstance suggests a further point. The expressions 'unrevealed God' and '*tremenda maiestas*' manifestly repeated only those 'moments' of the numinous which we found first in our analysis of it (p. 27), especially the *tremendum*, the *daunting* aspect of the numinous. What of that of 'fascination' in Luther? Is it missing altogether, to be replaced merely by the rational attributes of trustworthiness and love and the corresponding element in the mind of the worshipper, viz. faith and trustfulness? No, beyond all question it is not. Only, the element of fascination is in Luther wholly interwoven with these rational elements and comes to utterance with them and in them. This can be felt forcibly in the boisterous, almost Dionysiac, blissfulness of his experience of God.

Christians are a blissful people, who can rejoice at heart and sing praises, stamp and dance and leap for joy. That is well pleasing to God and doth our heart good, when we trust in God and find in Him our pride and our joyfulness. Such a gift should only kindle a fire and a light in our heart, so that we should never cease dancing and leaping for joy.

Who will extol this enough or utter it forth? It is neither to be expressed nor conceived.

If thou feelest it truly in the heart, it will be such a great thing to thee that thou wilt rather be silent than speak aught of it.[1]

Here should be borne in mind what was remarked earlier (pp. 61 ff.) respecting the interweaving of the non-rational with the rational and the consequently deepened import of rational expression. As the awe-inspiring character of the transcendent is comprised in the God of sternness and punishment and justice, so is its bliss-giving character included in the God who 'overbrims with pure goodness'. Indeed it is

1. Erlangen ed., xi. 194.

involved in the 'over-abounding' ('exuberant') and mystical tone of Luther's actual creed. Here, as elsewhere, there is no mistaking his connexion with mysticism. Though for Luther faith begins more and more to take the place of 'knowledge' and 'love of God' (*Gottes-Minne*) – which means a marked qualitative alteration of the whole religious temper, as compared with that of mysticism – yet, despite the change, it remains obvious that there are definite features in 'faith', as the term is used by Luther, which justify us in classing it with the mystical ways of response to which it is in apparent contrast, and clearly distinguish it from the *fides* taught by the Lutheran school with its determinate, well-ordered, unmystical temper. 'Faith' for Luther plays the same essential part, *mutatis mutandis*, as 'knowledge' and 'love' for the earlier mystics: it is the unique power of the soul, the *adhaesio Dei*, which *unites* man with God; and 'unity' is the very signature of the mystical. So that when Luther says that faith makes man 'one cake' (*ein Kuche*) with God or Christ, or holds him 'as a ring holds a jewel' (*sicut annulus gemmam*), he is not speaking any more figuratively than when Tauler says the same of love. 'Faith' for Luther, as 'love' for Tauler and the mystics generally, is a something that cannot be exhaustively comprised in rational concepts, and to designate which 'figures' and 'images' are a necessity. To him 'faith' is the centre of the soul – the *fundus animae* or 'basis of the soul' of the mystics – in which the union of man with God fulfils itself. It is at the same time an independent faculty of knowledge, a mystical *a priori* element in the spirit of man, by which he receives and recognizes supra-sensible truth, and in this respect identical with the 'Holy Spirit in the heart' (*Spiritus Sanctus in corde*). 'Faith' is further the 'mighty creative thing' in us and the strongest of *affects*, most closely akin to the Greek 'enthusiasm' (ἐνθουσιά-ζεσθαι). It even takes over all the functions which all 'enthusiasts' from Paul onwards have ascribed to 'the Spirit'; for it is 'faith' that 'transforms us inwardly and brings us forth anew'. In this regard, different as it is in its inner attitude, 'faith' is very similar to the *amor mysticus*. And in the bliss of the 'assurance of salvation' (*certitudo salutis*) that it arouses, and the intensity of Luther's 'childlike faith', we have in a subdued form a recurrence of the 'childhood' feelings of Paul, which go beyond mere comfort of the soul, appeasement of conscience, or feeling of protectedness. All subsequent mystics from Johann Arndt to Spener and Arnold[1] have always felt these aspects of Luther's inner life to be congenial and akin to their own, and have carefully collected the relevant passages from his writings as a defence against the attacks of the rationalized doctrine of the Lutheran school.

For in opposition to the 'rationalizations' of the schools the non-rational elements are maintained and fostered in the Western mysticism that came to its later flower both on Catholic and Protestant soil. In this, as in Christian mysticism as a whole from its first stirrings, the elements of the non-rational already detailed are easily recognizable, most prominently of all those of 'mystery', 'fascination', and 'majesty'. The element of 'awe', on the other hand, recedes and is subdued; there has never been in the West a mysticism of horror, such as we find in certain kinds of Indian mysticism, both Buddhist and Hindu – in Bhagavad-Gītā, ch. 11 – in some forms of the Shiva and Durgā worship, and in the horrible form of Tantrism. Yet, though the *tremendum* element in Christian mysticism is subdued, it is not entirely lacking. It remains a living factor in the *caligo* and the *altum silentium*, in the 'abyss', the 'night', the 'deserts' of the divine nature, into which the soul must descend, in the 'agony', 'abandonment', 'barrenness', *taedium*, in which it must tarry, in the shuddering and shrinking from the loss and deprivation of selfhood and the 'annihilation' of personal identity. Thus Suso writes:

In this inconceivable mountain of the supra-divine Where [the 'height of the divine Majesty transcending substance'] there is a precipitousness of which all pure spirits are sensible. Here the Soul enters a secret namelessness, a marvellous alienation. It is the bottomless abyss no creature can sound – . . . the spirit

1. [Johann Arndt, 1555–1621; Gottfried Arnold, 1666–97; Philipp Jacob Spener, 1635–1705: the last-named was one of the founders of 'Pietism' in Germany. (*Trans.*)]

perishes there, to become all-living in the wonders of the God-head.[1]

And he can pray:

Ah, woe is me, Thy wrathful countenance is so full of fury. Thy turning away in anger is so unendurable. Woe is me! And the words of Thy enmity are so fiery, they cleave through heart and soul.[2]

This note is familiar also to the later mystics. Thus St John of the Cross says:

As this clear sight of the divine comes like a violent assault upon the soul to subdue it, the soul feels such anguish in its weakness that all power and breath leave it together, while sense and spirit as though they stood burdened beneath a dark unmeasured load suffer such agony and are oppressed by such deadly fear that the soul would choose death as a mitigation and refreshment.[3]

And again:

The fourth kind of anguish is brought into being in the soul . . . from the Majesty and Glory of God.[2]

Once more:

Therefore He destroys, crushes and overwhelms (the soul) in such a deep darkness, that it feels as though melted and in its misery destroyed by a cruel death of the spirit. Even as though it were to feel it had been swallowed by some savage beast and buried in the darkness of his belly.[3]

But in our Western mysticism the writer in whom the non-rationally 'dreadful' and even the 'daemonic' phase of the numinous remains a most living element is Jacob Boehme. For all his adoption of its motives, Boehme is in his speculation and 'theosophy' sharply distinguished from the earlier mysticism. He is at one with this (as represented, for instance, by Eckhart) in aiming at a 'construction' and an understanding of God, and

1. Suso, German writings, ed. Denifle, pp. 289 ff.
2. Ibid., p. 353.
3. St John of the Cross, *The Ascent of Mount Carmel.*

from Him of the world: and, like Eckhart, he finds as a starting-point for his speculation the 'primal bottom', the supra-comprehensible and inexpressible. But this stands to him, not for Being and Above-being, but for Stress and Will; it is not good and above-good, but a supra-rational identification of good and evil in an Indifferent, in which is to be found the potentiality for evil as well as for good, and therewith the possibility of the dual nature of deity itself as at once goodness and love on the one hand and fury and wrath on the other.[1] If the inventions and comparisons, with whose aid Boehme composes a sort of chemico-physical romance of God, strike us as extremely queer and bizarre, the strange intuitions of the religious feeling underlying them are yet highly significant. They are intuitions of the numinous, and are akin to those of Luther. With Boehme, as with Luther, the non-rational energy and majesty of God and his 'awefulness' appear conceptualized and symbolized as 'Will'. And with Boehme, as with Luther, this is conceived as fundamentally independent of *moral* elevation or righteousness, and as indifferent toward good or evil action. It is rather a 'ferocity', a 'fiery wrath' about something unknown; or, better still, not about anything at all, but Wrath on its own account and without reference to any object; an aspect of character which would be quite meaningless if

1. The 'ferocity' is the origin of Lucifer, in whom the mere potentiality of evil is actualized. It might be said that Lucifer is 'fury', the ὀργή, hypostatized, the *mysterium tremendum* cut loose from the other elements and intensified to *mysterium horrendum*. The roots at least of this may be found in the Bible and the early Church. The ideas of propitiation and ransom are not without reference to Satan as well as to the divine wrath. The rationalism of the myth of the 'fallen angel' does not render satisfactorily the horror of Satan and of the 'depths of Satan' (Rev. ii. 24) and the 'mystery of iniquity' (2 Thess. ii. 7). It is a horror that is in some sort numinous, and we might designate the object of it as the negatively numinous. This also holds good of other religions than that of the Bible. In all religions 'the devilish' plays its part and has its place as that which, opposed to the divine, has yet something in common with it. As such it should be the subject of a special inquiry, which must be an analysis of fundamental feelings, and something very different from a mere record of the 'evolution of the idea of the devil'.

taken literally in the sense of a real conceivable and apprehensible anger. Who is not directly conscious that it is simply the non-rational element of 'awefulness', the *tremendum*, for which 'wrath', 'fire', 'fury', are excellent ideograms?[1] If such an ideogram is taken as an adequate concept, the result is anthropomorphism, such as mythology illustrates, and the writings of Lactantius (see p. 112). And if speculation follows, based upon such concepts, the result is the pseudo-science of theosophy. For the characteristic mark of all theosophy is just this: having confounded analogical and figurative ways of expressing feeling with rational concepts, it then systematizes them, and out of them spins, like a monstrous web, a 'science of God', which is and remains something monstrous, whether it employs, as Eckhart, the doctrinal terms of scholasticism; or as Boehme, the alchemical substances and mixtures of Paracelsus; or as Hegel, the categories of an animistic logic; or as Mrs Besant, the elaborate diction of Indian religion. For the history of religion it is not on account of his theosophy that Boehme is interesting, but because in him behind the theosophy the consciousness of the numinous was astir and alive as an element of genuine value: so that herein Boehme was an heir of Luther, preserving what in Luther's own school came to be overlooked and disregarded.

For the Lutheran school has itself not done justice to the numinous side of the Christian idea of God. By the exclusively moral interpretation it gave to the terms, it distorted the meaning of 'holiness' and the 'wrath' of God, and already from the time of Johann Gerhardt and onwards Lutheranism was returning to the doctrine of divine ἀπάθεια or passionlessness. More and more it deprived the forms of worship of the genuinely contemplative and specifically 'devotional' elements in them. The conceptual and doctrinal – the ideal of orthodoxy – began

1. Boehme's disciple, Johann Pordage, has some feeling of this when he writes: 'So hope I then, that you will not be angered with me, if you find that I impute to God acerbity and bitterness, dread, wrath, fire, . . . and the like. For even Jacob Boehme found no other words in which to express his exalted *sensation* (*Empfindung*) of God. You must then take all those forms of speech in a high divine sense, far removed from all imperfection' (*Divine and True Metaphysic*, i. 166).

to preponderate over the inexpressible, whose only life is in the conscious mental attitude of the devout soul. The Church became a school, and her communications, in truth, found a more and more contracted access to the mind, as Tyrrell has put it somewhere, 'through the narrow clefts of the understanding'.

Schleiermacher was the first to attempt to overcome this rationalism, most boldly and uncompromisingly in the rhapsody of his *Discourses*, with less heat and more subdued tone in his *Glaubenslehre* and his theory of the 'feeling of absolute dependence', which in point of fact give a representation – as has been pointed out already – of the first stirring of the feeling of the numinous. It will be a task for contemporary Christian teaching to follow in his traces and again to deepen the rational meaning of the Christian conception of God by permeating it with its non-rational elements.

The Two Processes of Development

THIS permeation of the rational with the non-rational is to lead, then, to the deepening of our rational conception of God; it must not be the means of blurring or diminishing it. For if (as suggested at the close of the last chapter) the disregard of the numinous elements tends to impoverish religion, it is no less true that 'holiness', 'sanctity', as Christianity intends the words, cannot dispense with the rational, and especially the clear ethical elements of meaning which Protestantism more particularly emphasizes in the idea of God. To get the full meaning of the word 'holy' as we find it used in the New Testament (and religious usage has established it in the New Testament sense to the exclusion of others), we must no longer understand by 'the holy' or 'sacred' the merely numinous in general, nor even the numinous at its own highest development; we must always understand by it the numinous completely permeated and saturated with elements signifying rationality, purpose, personality, morality. It is in this combined meaning that we retain and apply the term 'holy' in our subsequent chapters. But that the course of the historical development may be clearly understood, we venture first to recapitulate our view upon this matter as explicitly as possible.

That which the primitive religious consciousness first apprehends in the form of 'daemonic dread', and which, as it further unfolds, becomes more elevated and ennobled, is in origin not something rational or moral, but something distinct, non-rational, an object to which the mind responds in a unique way with the special feeling-reflexes that have been described. And this element or 'moment' passes in itself through a process of development of its own, quite apart from the other process – which begins at an early stage – by which it is 'rationalized' and 'moralized', i.e. filled with rational and ethical meaning. Taking this non-rational process of development first, we have seen how the 'daemonic dread', after itself passing through various gradations, rises to the level of 'fear of the gods', and thence to 'fear of God'. The δαιμόνιον or daemonic power becomes the θεῖον or divine power: 'dread' becomes worship; out of a confusion of inchoate emotions and bewildered palpitations of feeling grows '*religio*', and out of 'shudder' a holy awe. The feelings of dependence upon and beatitude in the numen, from being relative, become absolute. The false analogies and fortuitous associations are gradually dispelled or frankly rejected. The numen becomes God and Deity. It is then to God and Deity, as 'numen' rendered absolute, that the attribute, denoted by the terms *qādôsh, sanctus, ἅγιος*, holy, pertains, in the first and directest sense of the words. It is the culmination of a development which works itself out purely in the sphere of the non-rational. This development constitutes the first central fact of religious study, and it is the task of religious history and psychology to trace its course.

Next, secondary and subsidiary to this, is the task of tracing the course of the process of rationalization and moralization *on the basis of* the numinous consciousness. It nearly, if not quite, synchronizes and keeps pace with the stages of the purely numinous development, and, like that, it can be traced in its different gradations in the most widely different regions of religious history. Almost everywhere we find the numinous attracting and appropriating meanings derived from social and individual ideals of obligation, justice, and goodness. These become the 'will' of the numen, and the numen their guardian, ordainer, and author. More and more these ideas come to enter into the very essence of the numen and charge the term with ethical content. 'Holy' becomes 'good', and 'good' from that very fact in turn becomes 'holy', 'sacrosanct'; until there results a thenceforth indissoluble synthesis of the two elements, and the final outcome is thus the fuller, more complex sense of 'holy', in which it is at once *good and sacrosanct*. The greatest distinction of the religion of ancient Israel, at least from Amos onwards, is precisely the intimate coalescence of both elements. No God is like the God of Israel: for He is the absolutely Holy One (= perfectly good). And, on the other hand, no law is like

Yahweh's Law, for it is not merely good, but also at the same time 'holy' (= sacrosanct).

And this process of rationalization and moralization of the numinous, as it grows ever more clear and more potent, is in fact the most essential part of what we call 'the History of Salvation' and prize as the ever-growing self-revelation of the divine. But at the same time it should be clear to us that this process of the 'moralization of the idea of God', often enough represented to us as a principal problem, setting the main line for inquiry into the history of religion, is in no wise a suppression of the numinous or its supersession by something else – which would result not in a God, but a God-substitute – but rather the completion and charging of it with a new content. That is to say, the 'moralization' process assumes the numinous and is only completed upon this as basis.

CHAPTER XII

The Holy as an *A Priori* Category

PART I

IT follows from what has been said that the 'holy' in the fullest sense of the word is a combined, complex category, the combining elements being its rational and non-rational components. But in *both* – and the assertion must be strictly maintained against all sensationalism and naturalism – it is a *purely a priori* category.

The rational ideas of absoluteness, completion, necessity, and substantiality, and no less so those of the good as an objective value, objectively binding and valid, are not to be 'evolved' from any sort of sense-perception. And the notions of 'epigenesis', 'heterogony', or whatever other expression we may choose to denote our compromise and perplexity, only serve to conceal the problem, the tendency to take refuge in a Greek terminology being here, as so often, nothing but an avowal of one's own insufficiency. Rather, seeking to account for the ideas in question, we are referred away from all sense-experience back to an original and underivable capacity of the mind implanted in the 'pure reason' independently of all perception.

But in the case of the non-rational elements of our category of the Holy we are referred back to something still deeper than the 'pure reason', at least as this is usually understood, namely, to that which mysticism has rightly named the *fundus animae*, the 'bottom' or 'ground of the soul' (*Seelengrund*). The ideas of the numinous and the feelings that correspond to them are, quite as much as the rational ideas and feelings, absolutely 'pure', and the criteria which Kant suggests for the 'pure' concept and the 'pure' feeling of respect are most precisely applicable to them. In the famous opening words of the *Critique of Pure Reason* he says:

That all our knowledge begins with experience there can be

no doubt. For how is it possible that the faculty of cognition should be awakened into exercise otherwise than by means of objects which affect our senses? . . . But, though all our know-ledge begins *with* experience, it by no means follows that all arises *out of* experience.

And, referring to empirical knowledge, he distinguishes that part which we receive through impressions and that which our own faculty of cognition supplies from itself, *sense-impressions giving merely the occasion.*

The numinous is of the latter kind. It issues from the deepest foundation of cognitive apprehension that the soul possesses, and, though it of course comes into being in and amid the sensory data and empirical material of the natural world and cannot anticipate or dispense with those, yet it does not arise *out of* them, but only *by their means*. They are the incitement, the stimulus, and the 'occasion' for the numinous experience to become astir, and, in so doing, to begin – at first with a naïve immediacy of reaction – to be interfused and interwoven with the present world of sensuous experience, until, becoming gradually purer, it disengages itself from this and takes its stand in absolute contrast to it. The proof that in the numinous we have to deal with purely *a priori* cognitive elements is to be reached by introspection and a critical examination of reason such as Kant instituted. We find, that is, involved in the numinous experience, beliefs and feelings qualitatively different from anything that 'natural' sense-perception is capable of giving us. They are themselves not perceptions at all, but peculiar interpretations and valuations, at first of perceptual data, and then – at a higher level – of posited objects and entities, which themselves no longer belong to the perceptual world, but are thought of as supple-menting and transcending it. And as they are not themselves sense-perceptions, so neither are they any sort of 'transmuta-tion' of sense-perceptions. The only 'transmutation' possible in respect to sense-perception is the transformation of the in-tuitively given concrete percept, of whatever sort, into the corresponding concept; there is never any question of the transformation of *one* class of percepts into a class of entities qualitatively *other*. The facts of the numinous consciousness point therefore – as likewise do also the 'pure concepts of the understanding' of Kant and the ideas and value-judgements of ethics or aesthetics – to a hidden substantive source, from which the religious ideas and feelings are formed, which lies in the mind independently of sense-experience; a 'pure reason' in the profoundest sense, which, because of the 'surpassingness' of its content, must be distinguished from both the pure theoretical and the pure practical reason of Kant, as something yet higher or deeper than they.

The justification of the 'evolutionist' theory of to-day stands or falls with its claim to 'explain' the phenomenon of religion. That is in truth the real task of the psychology of religion. But in order to explain we must have the data from which an explanation may be forthcoming; out of nothing nothing can be explained. Nature can only be explained by an investigation into the ultimate fundamental forces of nature and their laws: it is meaningless to propose to go farther and explain these laws themselves, for in terms of what are they to be explained? But in the domain of spirit the corresponding principle from which an explanation is derived is just the spirit itself, the reasonable spirit of man, with its predispositions, capacities, and its own inherent laws. This has to be presupposed: it cannot itself be explained. None can say how mind or spirit 'is made' – though this is in effect just what the theory of epigenesis is fain to attempt. The history of humanity begins with man, and we have to presuppose man, to take him for granted as he is, in order that from him we may understand his history. That is, we must presuppose man as a being analogous to ourselves in natural propensities and capacities. It is a hopeless business to seek to lower ourselves into the mental life of a *pithecanthropus erectus*; and, even if it were not, we should still need to start from man as he is, since we can only interpret the psychical and emotional life of animals regressively by clumsy analogies drawn from the developed human mind. To try, on the other hand, to understand and deduce the human from the sub-human or brute mind is to try to fit the lock to the key instead of vice versa; it is to seek to illuminate light by darkness. In the first appearance of conscious life on dead unconscious matter we have a simple, irreducible, inexplicable datum. But that which here appears is already a manifold of qualities, and we can only interpret it as a seed of potentiality, out of which issue continually maturer powers and capacities, as the organization of the body increases in stability and complexity. And the only way we can throw any light upon the whole region of sub-human psychical life is by interpreting it once again as a sort of 'predisposition'[1] at a second remove, i.e. a predisposition to form the predispositions or faculties of the actual developed mind, and standing in relation to this as an embryo to the full-grown organism. But we are not completely in the dark as to the meaning of this word 'predisposition'.[1] For in our own awakening and growth to mental and spiritual maturity we trace in ourselves in some sort the evolution by which the seed develops into the tree – the very opposite of 'transformation' and 'epigenesis' by successive addition.[2]

We call the source of growth a hidden 'predisposition' of the human spirit, which awakens when aroused by divers excitations. That there are 'predispositions' of this sort in individuals no one can deny who has given serious study to the history of religion. They are seen as propensities, 'predestining' the individual to religion, and they may grow spontaneously to quasi-instinctive presentiments, uneasy seeking and groping, yearning and longing, and become a religious *impulsion*, that

---

1. *Anlage.*
2. The physical analogue to these spiritual or mental relationships is the relation of potential to kinetic energy. The assumption of such a relation in the world of mind (i.e. a relation between potential and kinetic mind) is, of course, only to be expected from one who is prepared to accept as the final cause of all mind in the world as a whole the absolute mind as 'pure actuality' whose *ellampatio* or effulgence (in Leibniz's phrase) all other mind is. For all that is potential presupposes an *actual* as the ground of its possibility, as Aristotle long ago showed. But indeed how can we afford to reject such a 'pure actuality'? It is an inconsequent proceeding to postulate actuality, as is done, for a starting-point for the physical world, as a system of stored-up energy, whose transference to kinetic energy constitutes the 'rush of worlds and wheel of systems', and yet to reject the analogous assumption in the world of mind and spirit.

only finds peace when it has become clear to itself and attained its goal. From them arise the states of mind of 'prevenient grace', described in masterly fashion by Suso:

Loving, tender Lord! My mind has from the days of my childhood sought something with an earnest thirst of longing, Lord, and what that is have I not yet perfectly apprehended. Lord, I have now for many a year been in hot pursuit of it, and never yet have I been able to succeed, for I know not aright what it is. And yet it is something that draws my heart and my soul after it, and without which I can never attain to full repose. Lord, I was fain in the earliest days of my childhood to seek it among created things, as I saw others before me do. And the more I sought, the less I found it; and the nearer I went, the further I wandered from it. . . . Now my heart rages for it, for fain would I possess it. . . . Woe is me! . . . What is this, or how is it fashioned, that plays within me in such hidden wise?[1]

These are manifestations of a *predisposition* becoming a search and a driving *impulsion*. But here, if nowhere else, the 'fundamental biogenetic law' really does hold good, which uses the stages and phases in the growth of the individual to throw light upon the corresponding stages in the growth of his species. The *predisposition* which the human reason brought with it when the species Man entered history became long ago, not merely for individuals but for the species as a whole, a *religious impulsion*, to which incitements from without and pressure from within the mind both contributed. It begins in undirected, groping emotion, a seeking and shaping of representations, and goes on, by a continual onward striving, to generate ideas, till its nature is self-illumined and made clear by an explication of the obscure *a priori* foundation of thought itself, out of which it originated.[2] And this emotion, this searching, this generation and explication of ideas, gives the warp of the fabric of religious evolution, whose woof we are to discuss later.[3]

1. *Works*, ed. Denifle, p. 311.

2. The reader may compare what Kant says in his *Lectures on Psychology* (Leipzig ed., 1889, p. 11) of 'the treasure buried in the field of obscure ideas, constituting the deep abyss of human knowledge, which we cannot sound'. This 'deep abyss' is just the *fundus animae* that is aroused in Suso.　　　　　　　　　　　3. Cf. pp. 194, 195.

CHAPTER XIII

Its Earliest Manifestations

ONLY upon the basis of the foregoing assumptions is it possible to understand the historical origin and further development of religion. It must be admitted that when religious evolution first begins sundry curious phenomena confront us, preliminary to religion proper and deeply affecting its subsequent course. Such are the notions of 'clean' and 'unclean', belief in and worship of the dead, belief in and worship of 'souls' or 'spirits', magic, fairy tale, and myth, homage to natural objects, whether frightful or extraordinary, noxious or advantageous, the strange idea of 'power' (*orenda* or *mana*), fetishism and totemism, worship of animal and plant, daemonism and polydaemonism. Different as these things are, they are all haunted by a common – and that a numinous – element, which is easily identifiable. They did not, perhaps, take their origin out of this common numinous element directly; they may have all exhibited a preliminary stage at which they were merely 'natural' products of the naïve, rudimentary fancies of primitive times. But these things acquire a strand of a quite special kind, which alone gives them their character as forming the vestibule of religion, brings them first to clear and explicit form, and furnishes them with the prodigious power over the minds of men which history universally proves them to possess. Let us attempt to grasp this peculiar strand, common to all these modes of thought and practice which stand upon the threshold of religion.

1. We will begin with *magic*. There has been at all times, and there still is to-day, a 'natural' magic, that is to say, modes of behaviour exhibiting some simple analogy and carried out quite unreflectively and without any basis in theory, whose object is to influence and regulate an event in accordance with the wishes of the agent. It may be noticed on any skittle-alley or bowling-green. A bowler aims and plays

his bowl, wishing it to run true and hit the jack. He watches eagerly as it rolls, nodding his head, his body bent sideways, stands balancing on one leg, jerks over violently to the other side as the critical point is reached, makes as though to push the ball on with hand or foot, gives a last jerk – and the end is reached. Its hazards past, the ball rolls safely into position. What was the man doing in this case? He was not simply imitating the course of the ball; he meant to prescribe and determine it, but this obviously without any reflection on his queer behaviour, without the belief of primitive man in 'universal animism', i.e. in the animatedness of everything, in this instance, of the ball, and without a belief in some sympathetic *rapport* between his own 'soul' power and the 'soul' of the ball. His action was merely naïvely analogical, for the attainment of a definite wish. The proceedings of 'rain-makers' were often, perhaps at first were always, just the same sort of thing; and so were the naïve charms purporting to influence the course of sun and moon, clouds and winds. But clearly, so long as they are not more than this, these are not by any means *magic* in the proper sense. There must be in addition a new ingredient, unique in quality, the element that is usually called 'supernatural efficacy'. But this expression is a misnomer: 'supernatural' has nothing to do with the case; it is much too imposing an expression, and ascribes far too much to the naïve mind. The conception of Nature as a single connected system of events united by laws is the final and most difficult outcome of abstraction; and this conception of nature, or at least some hint of it, must have been arrived at before there could be any place for its negation, the 'supernatural'. Again, nothing is explained, as Wundt would have it, by 'spirit-power' or 'soul-power'. For, first, it is to-day universally recognized that magic is independent of a belief in spirits or souls, and probably existed before it. And, second, the point at issue is not by means of what *class* of powers the magical effect was produced – whether 'soul-powers' or others – but by means of what *quality* or *character* in the powers. And this quality can be indicated solely through the 'daemonic', a character ascribed to certain definite operations of force, be they strong or weak, extraordinary or quite trivial, the work of a soul or a 'non-soul'. The quality can be only suggested through that unique element of feeling, the feeling of 'uncanniness', of which we have already spoken, whose positive content cannot be defined conceptually, and can only be indicated by that mental response to it which we called 'shuddering'.

2. The same is true of the *worship of the dead*. It does not arise out of any theory of animism, according to which the primitive man thinks of inanimate objects, and so also of the dead, as animate and operative. Even in itself this entire theory of an ostensible attribution of 'soul' or the principle of animation to everything is a mere fabrication of the study. How much more when it is clumsily spatchcocked and welded together with 'belief in spirits or souls', which is something quite different! The dead man, in point of fact, exercises a spell upon the mind only when, and only because, he is felt as a thing of horror and 'shudder'. But alike to the naïve mind of the savage and to the blasé mind of modern civilized man this feeling comes about with such an immediate compelling force that we usually accept it as something immediately self-evident, failing altogether to remark that even the estimating something as 'horrible' or 'grisly' shows the emergence of a qualitatively separate content of feeling which the mere fact of death does not explain. Feeling-reactions to the dead, if prompted 'naturally', are pretty obviously only of two kinds: on the one hand, the experient feels disgust at the corpse's putrefaction, stench, revoltingness: on the other, he feels his own will to life disturbed and checked, the fear of death and the startled fright that directly follows on the sight of a corpse, especially if it be that of a member of one's own species. Both these sorts of feeling-response, viz. disgust and startled fright, are already found manifested among animals. I observed this in a very pronounced degree on one occasion, when, upon a lonely ride, we suddenly came upon the body of a dead horse, and Diana, my excellent mount, on recognizing her dead fellow, gave every indication of the most natural fright and disgust. But these two 'moments' of feeling do not by any

means afford in themselves the materials for the 'art of making shudder' (in the words of the old folk-tale). It is something new and demands to be 'learnt' as the folk-tale rightly declares: that is, this is a feeling that is not simply present with the other 'natural' and normal mental functions, disgust, or fright, and cannot be got from these by analysis. It is a 'dread' (or awe), qualitatively *sui generis*; and even with regard to this rudimentary stage represented by the primitive 'worship of the dead' we cannot admit that we have to do merely with a universal feeling, that has simply to be presupposed at the outset as a regular factor of folk psychology, a collectively engendered feeling that explains itself. On the contrary, it cannot be disputed that here too there have been persons endowed with special propensities in this direction, who possessed such feelings actually, and then, by giving expression to them, aroused them in others. Even the 'awe of the dead' and from it the 'worship of the dead' have been, as it were, 'instituted' and have had 'founders'.

3. We consider next ideas of '*souls*' and '*spirits*'. It would be possible to show, did not the subject lead us too far afield, that these were not conceived by the fanciful processes of which the animists tell us, but had a far simpler origin. But again the important point is not the origin of 'spirits' in their ideational aspect, but the qualitative element of feeling relative to them. And this does not consist in the fact that 'spirits' or 'souls' are thinner or less easily visible than the body, or quite invisible, or fashioned like air: often all this is true of them; no less often none of it is; most frequently of all it is both true and false. The essence of the 'soul' lies *not* in the imaginative or conceptual expression of it, but first and foremost in the fact that it is a *spectre*; that it arouses 'dread' or 'awe', as described above. But again, a 'spectre' is not to be explained from 'natural' feelings, and these are equally unable to explain the further development by which these 'something' (and this is the only core of conceptual meaning that can really be given them), at first always very eagerly shunned, later on become beings honoured in a positive way and loved, capable of rising into heroes, *pitris*, daemons, holy or sacred ones, and gods.

4. We turn to the idea of '*power*', the *mana* of the Pacific Islands and the *orenda* of the North American Indians. It can have its antecedents in very 'natural' phenomena. To notice power in plants, stones, and natural objects in general and to appropriate it by gaining possession of them; to eat the heart or liver of an animal or a man in order to make his power and strength one's own – this is not religion but science. Our science of medicine follows a similar prescription. If the 'power' of a calf's glands is good for goitre and imbecility, we do not know what virtue we may not hope to find in frogs' brains or Jews' livers. All depends here upon observation, and our science of medicine in this respect only differs from that of the medicine-man in being more exact and in possessing experimental methods. 'Power' does not take its place in the antechamber of religion, is not appropriated by religion in 'communion rites' and 'sacraments' (as we call them), until it too has come to include the idea of 'spell' and 'magic'.

5. Volcanoes, mountain peaks, moon, sun, and clouds are regarded by primitive man as being *alive* or *animate*, not in consequence of a naïve theory of the omnipresence of 'spirit' or 'soul' – 'panthelism', so called – but as a result of precisely the same criterion that we ourselves apply when we recognize anything to be alive or animate, apart from the one live thing we can observe directly, our self; that is to say, both we and the primitive credit an object with life if, and in so far as, we think we remark in it living efficacy and agency; and whether we do so rightly or wrongly is again simply a matter of more or less exact observation. But while from this criterion the natural objects mentioned above, and of course others, may be invested with life by the naïve observer, this does *not* in itself lead to myth or religion. Purely as *animate* or living beings, these entities are far from being yet 'divine' or 'gods'; nay, they do not even become so when the man turns to them with desire and petition; for petition is something less than prayer, and trust need not have a religious character. The objects in question only become 'divine' – objects of *worship* – when the category of the numinous is applied to them, and that does not come about until, first, an attempt is made to *influence* them by

numinous means, viz. by magic; and, second, their special efficacy or way of working is at the same time accepted as something numinous, viz. something magical.

6. As regards *fairy-stories*, these presuppose the 'natural' impulse to fantasy, narrative, and entertainment, and its products. But the fairy-story proper only comes into being with the element of the 'wonderful', with miracle and miraculous events and consequences, i.e. by means of an infusion of the numinous. And the same holds good in an increased degree of *myth*.

7. All the factors and elements named so far in this chapter are but, as it were, the vestibule at the threshold of the real religious feeling, an earliest stirring of the numinous consciousness, which comes upon the scene blended with associated feelings in conformity to principles of analogy which it would be easy to specify for each several case. Only with the rise of the '*daemon*' do we have a really separate beginning. The most authentic form of the 'daemon' may be seen in those strange deities of ancient Arabia, which are properly nothing but wandering demonstrative pronouns, neither 'given shape and feature by means of myth', for there is in the main no mythology attached to them at all, nor 'evolved out of nature-deities', nor grown out of 'souls' or 'spirits', but none the less felt as deities of mighty efficacy, who are the objects of very living veneration. They are pure products of the religious consciousness itself. And in their case it is very evident that they do not arise as a collective product of crowd-imagination, and that they do not therefore have their origin in 'group-' or 'folk-' psychology, but were the intuitions of persons of innate prophetic powers. For there is always the *kāhin* (the primitive form of the 'prophet') belonging to these numina, and he alone experiences a numen or divine-daemonic power at first hand. Only where and when it has been 'revealed' through such a one do the forms of worship and a common cult arise. To each numen is assigned a seer and there is none without one.

8. The notions 'clean' and 'unclean', 'pure' and 'impure', are already found in a purely natural sense, prior to their religious application. The unclean is the loathsome, that which stirs

strong feelings of natural disgust. And it is just during the more primitive stages of human development that the emotion of disgust exercises such special power. Probably these emotional reactions are a part of our natural self-protective endowment, instinctive safeguards for many important vital functions. The effect of civilization is to refine these emotions of disgust and loathing by diverting them to different objects, so that things which were loathsome to the savage cease to be so and things which were not become so. This refinement spells at the same time a weakening in the intensity of the emotion; we do not now *loathe* and feel disgust with the unbridled violence and strength of the savage. In this respect we can notice even to-day a plain distinction between our more primitive rural and our more 'refined' urban population: we townsmen feel disgust at much that is harmless to the countryman, but where the latter does feel it he is affected by the emotion more radically than we are; it is a profounder reaction in him.

We have so far been concerned with the ordinary feeling of disgust. Between this and the feeling of the 'horrible' there is a very close analogy; and from this it becomes apparent, in accordance with the law of reciprocal attraction between analogous feelings and emotions, how the 'natural' unclean or impure is bound to pass over into, and develop in, the sphere of the numinous. Once, in fact, we have in our hand the key of the problem – the analogy and the law just mentioned – we can reconstruct *a priori* the actual genetic process involved, by which the one emotion prompts the other. We indeed have ourselves a direct experience of the same thing to-day in our emotional reaction to the sight of flowing blood, in which it would be hard to say whether the element of 'disgust' or 'horror' is the stronger.

Later, then, when the more maturely developed elements of 'awe' came upon the scene and went to shape the more elevated ideas of the daemonic and the divine, *sacer* and *sanctus*, things could become 'unclean' or 'impure' in the numinous sense without any substratum of 'natural' impurity to serve as point of departure. And we can learn something of the relation of feeling-analogy involved from the fact that in the reverse

direction the feeling of the *numinously* impure calls up easily
by association the 'natural' emotion of disgust (i.e. the feeling
of the 'naturally' impure), so that things become disgustful or
loathsome which intrinsically were not objects of disgust at all,
but of numinous horror. In fact such secondary and derived
feelings of disgust can maintain themselves independently long
after the original numinous awe which they once evoked has
died away. Certain *social* feelings of loathing, such as those of
caste, can be explained in this way: they had once a purely
daemonic root, but long after that has died out they still survive
in their secondary, acquired character as feelings of disgust.

9. If the examples numbered 1 to 8 may be termed 'pre-
religion', this is not in the sense that religion and the possibility of religion are explicable by their means: rather, they
are themselves only made possible and can only be explained
from a religious basic element, viz. the feeling of the numinous.
This is a primal element of our psychical nature that needs to
be grasped purely in its uniqueness and cannot itself be explained from anything else. Like all other primal psychical
elements, it *emerges* in due course in the developing life of
human mind and spirit and is thenceforward simply present.
Of course it can only emerge if and when certain conditions are
fulfilled, conditions involving a proper development of the
bodily organs and the other powers of mental and emotional
life in general, a due growth in suggestibility and spontaneity
and responsiveness to external impressions and internal experiences. But such conditions are no more than conditions;
they are not its causes or constituent elements. To recognize
this is not to relegate the whole matter to the domain of mystery
and supernaturalism, but simply to maintain that the same
thing holds good of this which holds good of all other primal
elements of our mental or spiritual life. Pleasure or pain, love
or hate, all faculties of sense-perception, such as susceptibility
to light and sound, consciousness of space and time, and
subsequently all higher capacities of the mind, all duly emerge,
sooner or later, in the course of development. That they do so
in conformity to laws and under definite conditions is indis-
putable, but each is none the less a new, original, underivable

fact, and they are only to be 'explained' on the assumption of a rich potentiality of spirit or mind, which underlies the course of their development and realizes itself more and more abundantly in them in proportion as the conditions of organic and cerebral evolution are more fully realized. And what is true of all these other elements of our mental life is also true of the feeling of the numinous.

10. The purest case, however, of the spontaneous stirring of numinous emotion would seem to be that mentioned in No. 7 (the feeling of daemons), which is of quite special significance for the evolution of religion. This is because here the 'religious' emotion does not from the first get diverted (following the 'stimulation' of emotional associations) to earthly things, wrongly taken as numinous: but either it remains a pure feeling, as in 'panic' terror (in the literal sense of the word), or itself invents, or, better, discovers, the numinous object by rendering explicit the obscure germinal ideas latent in itself. Even this latter case is not altogether beyond the reach of introspective analysis, which, moreover, can throw some light upon the transition from mere feeling to its 'explication' and to the positing of the numinous object. At least there is none of us who has any living capacity for emotion but must have known at some time or at some place what it is to feel really 'uncanny', to have a feeling of 'eeriness'. And more exact psychological analysis will notice the following points in such a state of mind. First, there is the point of which we have already spoken, its separate and underivable, irreducible, qualitative character. Second, there is the very curious circumstance that the external features occasioning this state of mind are often quite slight, indeed so scanty that hardly any account can be given of them, so disproportionate are they to the strength of the emotional impression itself. Indeed the clutching force and violence of the emotion so far exceeds any impressiveness contributed by the circumstances of time and place that one can often scarcely speak of an 'impression' at all, but at most of an encounter, serving as cue or occasion for the felt experience. This experience of eerie shuddering and awe breaks out rather from depths of the soul which the circumstantial,

external impression cannot sound, and the force with which it breaks out is so disproportionate to the mere external stimulation that the eruption may be termed, if not entirely, at least very nearly, spontaneous. And with this we are brought to the third point which psychological analysis of the 'uncanny' experience brings to view: meanings are aroused and awakened in it of a unique and special content, though altogether obscure, latent, and germinal, which are the real ground for the emotion of awe. For, if such meanings are not there at the start in some form or other, the mental and emotional disturbance could never take place. In the fourth place, the mental state we are discussing may, on the one hand, remain pure 'feeling', pursue its course, and pass away without its obscure thought-content being rendered explicit. If in this implicit form it is summed up in a phrase, this will be merely some such exclamation as: 'How uncanny!' or 'How eerie this place is!' On the other hand, the implicit meaning may be rendered explicit. It is already a beginning of this explicative process – though still in merely negative terms – when a man says: '*It* is not quite right here'; '*It* is uncanny'. The English 'This place is haunted' shows a transition to a positive form of expression. Here we have the obscure basis of meaning and idea rising into greater clarity and beginning to make itself explicit as the notion, however vague and fleeting, of a transcendent Something, a real operative entity of a numinous kind, which later, as the development proceeds, assumes concrete form as a '*numen loci*', a daemon, an 'El', a Baal, or the like.

In Gen. xxviii. 17 Jacob says: 'How dreadful is this place! this is none other but the house of Elohim.' This verse is very instructive for the psychology of religion; it exemplifies the point that has just been made. The first sentence gives plainly the mental impression itself in all its immediacy, before reflection has permeated it, and before the meaning-content of the feeling itself has become clear or explicit. It connotes solely the *primal numinous awe*, which has been undoubtedly sufficient in itself in many cases to mark out 'holy' or 'sacred' places, and make of them spots of aweful veneration, centres of a cult admitting a certain development. There is no need, that is, for the experient to pass on to resolve his mere impression of the eerie and aweful into the idea of a 'numen', a divine power, dwelling in the 'aweful' place, still less need the *numen* become a *nomen*, a named power, or the '*nomen*' become something more than a mere pronoun. Worship is possible without this further explicative process. But Jacob's second statement gives this process of explication and interpretation; it is no longer simply an expression of the actual experience.

The German expression *Es spukt hier* (literally, it haunts here) is also instructive. It has properly no true subject, or at least it makes no assertion as to what the *es*, the 'it', is which 'haunts'; in itself it contains no suggestion of the concrete representations of 'ghost', 'phantom', 'spectre', or 'spirit' common to our popular mythology. Rather is the statement simply the pure expression of the emotion of 'eerieness' or 'uncanniness' itself, when just on the point of detaching and disengaging from itself a first vaguely intimated idea of a numinous something, an entity from beyond the borders of 'natural' experience. It is to be regretted that the German language possesses no general word less vulgar than 'spuken', no word which, instead of pointing us aside, as this word does, to the domain of superstition and the impure offshoots of the numinous consciousness, should retain its fundamental meaning in an unperverted form.[1] But even so we can feel by an effort of imaginative introjection how akin the debased feeling of haunting, given by this word, is to those primary numinous experiences by which long ago seers had experience of 'aweful', 'holy', numen-possessed places, discovering thereby the starting-points for local cults and the birth-places of the 'El' worshipped there. The echo of such primeval experiences lingers in Gen. xxviii. 17 (Jacob at Bethel) and Exod. iii (the

---

1. The expression *es geistet hier* may serve, but it has an artificial sound. The English 'to haunt' is a nobler expression than the German *spuken*. We might legitimately translate Hab. ii. 20: 'Yahweh haunts His holy Temple.' Such a 'haunting' is frequently the meaning of the Hebrew *shākan*. And we get a fuller and truer rendering of Ps. xxvi. 8: 'the place where thine honour-dwelleth' by translating it: 'the places haunted by Thy majesty'. The *Shekīnah* is properly the *haunting presence* of Yahweh in the Temple at Jerusalem.

burning bush). The places here set apart by Moses and Jacob are genuine 'haunted places', at which '*es spukt*', places about which 'there is something eerie'. Only, the feeling of being haunted has in these cases not the impoverished and debased sense of our modern eerie feeling of being haunted by ghosts and spectres; it comprises all the rich potentialities and possibilities of development inherent in the true primal numinous emotion. Nor can we doubt that even to-day the finer awe that may steal over us in the stillness and half-gloom of our own present-day sanctuaries has ultimate kinship not only with that of which Schiller writes in his verses:

> Und in Poseidons Fichtenhain
> Tritt er mit frommem Schauder ein,[1]

but also with genuine 'ghostly' emotions. The faint shiver that may accompany such states of mind is not unrelated to the feeling of 'creeping flesh', whose numinous character we have already considered (p. 29). In its efforts to derive 'daemon' and 'god' forcibly from 'souls' and 'spirits', animism is looking the wrong way. It would be, at any rate, on the right path if it maintained that they are haunting apparitions.

This is partially proved by certain ancient, still extant terms, which long ago had reference to the original awe of the haunting spirit (in the good sense), and later grew to become designations both of the lowest and the highest forms of 'awe'. Such a term is the enigmatical word *asura* in Sanskrit. *Asura* is the 'aweful' or 'dreadful' in the sense in which Jacob used the word, the eerie or uncanny. Later, in Indian religion, it is used as the technical expression for the lower forms of the spectral, ghostly, and daemonic. But at the same time it is from primeval times a title of the sublimest of all the gods of the Rig-Veda, the weirdly exalted *Varuna*. And in the Persian expression *Ahura-mazda* it becomes the name of the one and only eternal godhead itself. The same thing is true of the term *adbhuta*. You experience an *adbhuta* when you are 'in an empty house', says an old

[1]. Schiller. *Die Kraniche des Ibykus* (The Cranes of Ibykus):
'And to Poseidon's grove of pine
With awe devout he enters in.'

definition.[1] It is the experience of our 'shuddering'. But, on the other hand, *adbhuta* is also the name for the supreme transcendent marvel and its attractive spell, the element of 'fascination', even for the eternal Brahman himself and his salvation, the *Adbhutam* that passes beyond the reach of speech.[2]

11. Finally, it is only upon our assumption of an *a priori* basis of ideas and feelings that an explanation is forthcoming for the interesting phenomena to which Andrew Lang[3] rightly drew attention. These do not, of course, support the hypothesis of a 'primitive monotheism', that offspring of missionary apologetic, which eager to save the second chapter of Genesis yet feels the shame of a modern at the walking of Yahweh 'in the garden in the cool of the day'. But they do point to facts which remain downright riddles, if we start from any naturalistic foundation of religion – whether animism, pantheism, or another – and must in that case be got out of the way by the most violent hypotheses. The essence of the matter is this, that elements and strands are to be found in numerous mythologies and the stories of savage tribes, which reach altogether beyond the point they have otherwise attained in religious rites and usages. Notions of 'high gods' are adumbrated, with whom the savage has often hardly any relations in practice, if any at all, and in whom he yet acknowledges, almost in spite of himself, a value superior to that of all other mythological images, a value which may well accord with the divine in the highest sense.

Sometimes, but by no means always, we can discern that these anticipations of a higher religious experience are the outcome of a past growth of myth. What is characteristic and

1. *Adbhuta* means literally the inapprehensible, inexpressible. But in the first instance it is exactly our *mysterium stupendum*, whereas *asura* is the *tremendum*.

2. *Adbhuta* (and *āścarya*) would be an accurate rendering in Sanskrit for our 'numinous', were it not that the word, like the German *wunderbar* and the English 'awful', has long ago become trite and shallow from the 'profane' – non-religious – uses to which it has been so perpetually put.

3. *Myth, Ritual, and Religion*, 1899; *The Making of Religion*, 1902; *Magic and Religion*, 1901. Cf. also P. W. Schmidt. *Grundlinien einer Vergleichung der Religionen und Mythologien der austronesischen Völker*, Vienna, 1910.

at the same time so puzzling is the elevation with which they stand out from the surrounding more primitive religious life amid which they are found. Indeed, in cases where missions have introduced the preaching of Christian theism, these apprehended, exalted divinities are readily and frequently identified with God and reinforce the preaching of the missionary. And converts often come to admit that, though they had not honoured God, they had had knowledge of Him. It is, of course, true that this sort of fact can sometimes be explained as due to traditional influences, protracted from an earlier time, when the tribe in question was in contact with a higher theistic religion: the very names given to these higher beings sometimes prove as much. But even in this form the phenomenon is a very singular one. Why should 'savages', set in other respects in an utterly alien milieu of barbaric superstition, accept and, what is more, retain these notions, unless their own savage minds were so predisposed to them that, so far from being able to let them go, they were obliged to take at least an interest in them as a tradition and very frequently to acknowledge their authority by the felt witness of their own consciences? But, though the theory of a surviving tradition is sometimes applicable, there are many of these cases in which it is impossible to apply it without doing violence to the facts. In these we have clearly to do with anticipations and presentiments rather than survivals. Assuming the continual pressure and operation of an inward reasonable disposition to form certain ideas, these anticipations are not only no matter for surprise; they are as naturally to be expected as are the achievements of gipsy musicians, who, set otherwise in a milieu of the most primitive culture, yet respond to the pressure of a strong, innate, musical disposition. Without such an assumption the facts would remain as an insoluble puzzle.

Naturalistic psychologists, in this as in other cases, ignore a fact which might be thought at least to have a psychological interest, and which they could notice in themselves by careful introspection, namely, the *self-attestation* of religious ideas in one's own mind. This is, to be sure, more certain in the case of the naïve than in that of the more blasé mind; but many people would identify it in their own consciousness if they would only recall deliberately and impartially their hours of preparation for the ceremony of Confirmation. But what the mind 'attests' it can also under favourable circumstances evince and elicit from itself in premonitory stirring and felt surmise. The upholders of the theory of 'primitive mono-theism', on the other hand, show no less serious disregard of this central fact than the naturalistic psychologists. For if the phenomena we have been considering were based simply and solely on historical traditions and dim memories of a 'primeval revelation', as on such a theory they must be, this self-attestation from within would be just as much excluded as before.[1]

1. Compare with this chapter my recently published book *Das Gefühl des Überweltlichen*, especially Chapter VI: 'Das Werden eines Gottes.'

The 'Cruder' Phases

IT is not only the more developed forms of religious experience that must be counted underivable and *a priori*. The same holds good throughout and is no less true of the primitive, 'crude', and rudimentary emotions of 'daemonic dread' which, as we have seen, stand at the threshold of religious evolution. *Religion is itself present at its commencement*: religion, nothing else, is at work in these early stages of mythic and daemonic experience. Let us consider the circumstances in which alone the primitive and crude character of these consists.

(*a*) First, it is due to the merely gradual emergence and successive awakening of the several 'moments' of the numinous. The numinous only unfolds its full content by slow degrees, as one by one the series of requisite stimuli or incitements becomes operative. But where any whole is as yet incompletely presented its earlier and partial constituent moments or elements, aroused in isolation, have naturally something bizarre, unintelligible, and even grotesque about them. This is especially true of that religious moment which would appear to have been in every case the first to be aroused in the human mind, viz. daemonic dread. Considered alone and *per se*, it necessarily and naturally looks more like the opposite of religion than religion itself. If it is singled out from the elements which form its context, it appears rather to resemble a dreadful form of auto-suggestion, a sort of psychological nightmare of the tribal mind, than to have anything to do with religion; and the supernatural beings with whom men at this early stage profess relations appear as phantoms, projected by a morbid, undeveloped imagination afflicted by a sort of persecution-phobia. One can understand how it is that not a few inquirers could seriously imagine that 'religion' began with devil-worship, and that at bottom the devil is more ancient than God.

To this serial and gradual awakening of the different aspects and moments of the numinous is also to be ascribed the difficulty of classifying religions by genus and species. Everyone who undertakes the task produces a different classification. For the facts to be classified are for the most part not at all related as the distinct species of one and the same genus; they are not alternative, determinate forms into which the whole – 'religion' – may be analysed, but constituent elements, out of which it is to be 'synthesized' or built up. It is as though a whale should begin to show itself above the water part by part, and as though people should then attempt to classify the arched back, the end of the tail, and the head spouting water, by genus and species, instead of seeking for such a real understanding of these phenomena as would recognize each of them in its place and proper connexion with the rest as a part and member of *one* whole body, which must itself have been grasped in its entirety before its parts could be properly apprehended.

(*b*) In the second place, the 'primitiveness' of the cruder phases is due to the abrupt, capricious, and desultory character which marks the earliest form of numinous emotion; and, in consequence, to its indistinctness, which causes it to be merged and confounded with 'natural' feelings.

(*c*) It is due, next, to the fact that the valuation prompted by the moment of numinous consciousness (e.g. the 'daemonic dread' phase) is attached in the first place, and very naturally, to objects, occurrences, and entities falling within the workaday world of primitive experience, which prompt or give occasion to the stirring of numinous emotion by analogy and then divert it to themselves. This circumstance is more than anything else the root of what has been called nature-worship and the deification of natural objects. Only gradually, under pressure from the numinous feeling itself, are such connexions subsequently 'spiritualized' or ultimately altogether rejected, and not till then does the obscure content of the feeling, with its reference to absolute transcendent reality, come to light in all its integrity and self-subsistence.

(*d*) A fourth factor contributing to the crudity of primitive 'religion' is the uncontrolled, enthusiastic form, making for wild fanaticism, in which the numinous feeling storms the savage mind, appearing as religious mania, possession by the numen, intoxication, and frenzy.

(*e*) Again, a quite essential factor is the wrong schematizations it undergoes, when interpreted in terms of some experience analogous, perhaps, but not really appertaining to it. Examples of this have already been given (e.g. pp. 139–41).

(*f*) Finally, and most important, there is the deficient rationalization and moralization of the experience, for it is only gradually that the numinous feeling becomes charged with progressively rational, moral, and cultural significance.

These considerations account for the primitive and savage character of the numinous consciousness at its outset. But it must be repeated that in its content even the first stirring of 'daemonic dread' is a purely *a priori* element. In this respect it may be compared from first to last with the aesthetic judgement and the category of the beautiful. Utterly different as my mental experiences are when I recognize an object as 'beautiful' or as 'horrible', yet both cases agree in this, that I ascribe to the object an attribute that professes to interpret it, which I do not and cannot get from sense-experience, but which I rather ascribe to it by a spontaneous judgement of my own. Intuitively I apprehend in the object only its sensuous qualities and its spatial form, nothing more. That the *meaning* I call 'beautiful' fits the object, i.e. that these sense-data *mean* 'beautiful', or even that there *is* any such meaning at all – these are facts which sensory elements can in no wise supply or tell me. I must have an obscure conception of 'the beautiful itself', and, in addition, a principle of subsumption, by which I attribute it to the object, else even the simplest experience of a beautiful thing is rendered impossible. And this analogy may be pursued further. Joy in the beautiful, however analogous to mere pleasure in the agreeable, is yet distinguishable from it by a plain difference in quality, and cannot be derived from anything other than itself; and just such is the relation of the specific religious awe to mere natural fear.

The 'crude' stage is transcended as the numen reveals 'itself' (i.e. becomes manifest to mind and feeling) ever more strongly and fully. An essential factor in this is the process by which it is filled out and charged with rational elements, whereby it passes at the same time into the region of the conceivable and comprehensible. Yet all the time all the elements of non-rational 'inconceivability' are retained on the side of the numinous and intensified as the revelation proceeds. 'Revelation' does not mean a *mere* passing over into the intelligible and comprehensible. Something may be profoundly and intimately known in feeling for the bliss it brings or the agitation it produces, and yet the understanding may find no concept for it. To *know* and to *understand conceptually* are two different things, are often even mutually exclusive and contrasted. The mysterious obscurity of the numen is by no means tantamount to unknowableness. Assuredly the '*deus absconditus et incomprehensibilis*' was for Luther no '*deus ignotus*'. And so, too, St Paul 'knows' the peace, which yet 'passeth understanding'.

The Holy as an *A Priori* Category

PART II

WE conclude, then, that not only the rational but also the non-rational elements of the complex category of 'holiness' are *a priori* elements and each in the same degree. Religion is not in vassalage either to morality or teleology, *ethos* or *telos*, and does not draw its life from postulates; and its non-rational content has, no less than its rational, its own independent roots in the hidden depths of the spirit itself.

But the same *a priori* character belongs, in the third place, to the *connexion* of the rational and the non-rational elements in religion, their inward and necessary union. The histories of religion recount indeed, as though it were something axiomatic, the gradual interpenetration of the two, the process by which 'the divine' is charged and filled out with ethical meaning. And this process is, in fact, *felt* as something axiomatic, something whose inner necessity we feel to be self-evident. But then this inward self-evidence is a problem in itself; we are forced to assume an obscure, *a priori* knowledge of the necessity of this synthesis, combining rational and non-rational. For it is not by any means a *logical* necessity. How should it be logically inferred from the still 'crude', half-daemonic character of a moon-god or a sun-god or a numen attached to some locality, that he is a guardian and guarantor for the oath and of honourable dealing, of hospitality, of the sanctity of marriage, and of duties to tribe and clan? How should it be inferred that he is a god who decrees happiness and misery, participates in the concerns of the tribe, provides for its well-being, and directs the course of destiny and history? Whence comes this most surprising of all the facts in the history of religion, that beings, obviously born originally of horror and terror, become *gods* – beings to whom men pray, to whom they confide their sorrow or their happiness, in whom they behold the origin and the sanction of morality, law, and the whole canon of justice? And how does all this come about in such a way that, when once such ideas have been aroused, it is understood at once as the plainest and most evident of axioms, that so it must be?

Socrates, in Plato's *Republic*, ii. 382 E, says: 'God, then, is single and true in deed and word, and neither changes himself nor deceives others. . . .' And Adeimantos answers him: 'So too is it apparent to me, now that you say it.' The most interesting point in this passage is not the elevation and purity of the conception of God, nor yet the lofty rationalization and moralization of it here enunciated, but, on the side of Socrates, the apparently 'dogmatic' tone of his pronouncement – for he does not spend the least pains in demonstrating it – and, on the side of Adeimantos, the ingenuous surprise and, at the same time, the confident assurance with which he admits a truth novel to him. And his assent is such as implies convincement; he does not simply believe Socrates; he sees clearly for himself the truth of his words. Now this is the criterion of all *a priori* knowledge, namely, that, so soon as an assertion has been clearly expressed and understood, knowledge of its truth comes into the mind with the certitude of first-hand insight. And what passed here between Socrates and Adeimantos has been repeated a thousand times in the history of religions. Amos, also, says something new when he proclaims Yahweh as the God of inflexible, universal, and absolute righteousness, and yet this is a novelty that he neither proves nor justifies by an appeal to authorities. He appeals to *a priori* judgements, viz. to the religious conscience itself, and this in truth bears witness to his message.

Luther, again, recognizes and maintains such an *a priori* knowledge of the divine nature. His rage against the 'whore Reason' leads him, to be sure, usually to utterances in the opposite sense, such as the following:

It is a knowledge *a posteriori*, in that we look at God from without, at His works and His government, as one looketh at a castle or house from without and thereby feeleth (*spüret*) the lord or householder thereof. But *a priori* from within hath no wisdom of men yet availed to discover what and of what manner of being is God as He is in Himself or in His inmost essence, nor can any man know nor say aught thereof, but they to whom it has been revealed by the Holy Ghost.

Here Luther overlooks the fact that a man must 'feel' or detect the 'householder' *a priori* or not at all. But in other passages he himself allows the general human reason to possess many true cognitions of what 'God is in Himself or in His inmost essence'. Compare the following:

Atque ipsamet ratio naturalis cogitur eam concedere *proprio suo iudicio convicta*, etiamsi nulla esset scriptura. Omnes enim homines inveniunt hanc sententiam in cordibus suis scriptam et *agnoscunt* eam ac probatam, licet inviti, cum *audiant* eam tractari: primo, Deum esse omnipotentem . . . deinde, ipsum omnia nosse et praescire, neque errare neque falli posse. . . . Istis duobus corde et sensu concessis. . . .[1]

The interesting words of this statement are: *proprio suo iudicio convicta*, for they make the distinction between *cognitions* and mere 'innate ideas' or supernaturally instilled notions, both of which latter may produce 'thoughts', but not convictions '*ex proprio iudicio*'. Note also the words: 'cum *audiant* eam tractari', which exactly correspond to the experience of Plato's Adeimantos, already quoted.[2]

1. Luther, Weimar ed., xviii. 719: 'And the natural reason itself is forced even were there no holy scripture, to grant it (*sc.* this assertion), *convinced by its own judgement*. For all men, *as soon as they hear it treated of*, find this belief written in their hearts, and acknowledge it as proved, even unwillingly: first, that God is omnipotent, . . . then, that He has knowledge and foreknowledge of all things and can neither err nor be deceived. . . Since these two things are admitted by heart and feeling. . . .'

2. The most interesting features in Luther in this connexion, however, are the passages upon 'Faith', in which Faith is described as a unique cognitive faculty for the apprehension of divine truth, and as such is contrasted with the 'natural' capacities of the Understanding, as elsewhere the 'Spirit' is contrasted. 'Faith' is here like the 'Synteresis' in the theory of knowledge of the mystics, the 'inward teacher' (*magister internus*) of Augustine, and the 'inward light' of the Quakers, which are all of them of course 'above reason', but yet an *a priori*

It is the same experience which missionaries have so often undergone. Once enunciated and understood, the ideas of the unity and goodness of the divine nature often take a surprisingly short time to become firmly fixed in the hearer's mind, if he show any susceptibility for religious feeling. Frequently, thereupon, the hearer adapts the religious tradition that has hitherto been his to the new meaning he has

element in ourselves. A particularly striking passage is the following from Luther's *Table-Talk* (Wei. v. 5820):

'Omnium hominum mentibus impressa est divinitus notitia Dei. Quod sit Deus, omnes homines sine ulla artium et disciplinarum cognitione sola natura duce sciunt, et omnium hominum mentibus hoc divinitus impressum est. Nulla umquam fuit tam fera gens et immanis, quae non crediderit, esse divinitatem quandam, quae omnia creavit. Itaque Paulus inquit: Invisibilia Dei a creatura mundi per ea, quae facta sunt, intellecta conspiciuntur, sempiterna eius virtus et divinitas. Quare omnes ethnici sciverunt esse Deum, quantumvis fuerunt Epicurei, quantumvis contenderunt, non esse Deum. Non in eo, quod negant esse Deum, simul confessi sunt esse Deum? Nemo enim negare id potest, quod nescit. Quare, etsi quidam per omnem vitam in maximis versati sunt flagitiis et sceleribus et non aliter omnino vixerunt, ac si nullus esset Deus, tamen nunquam conscientiam animis potuerunt eicere testantem et affirmantem, quod sit Deus. Et quamvis illa conscientia pravis et perversis opinionibus ad tempus oppressa fuit, redit tamen et convincit eos in extremae vitae spiritu.'

'The knowledge of God is impressed upon the mind of every man by God. Under the sole guidance of nature all men know that God is – without any acquaintance with the arts or sciences; and this is divinely imprinted upon all men's minds. There has never been a people so wild and savage that it did not believe that there is some divine power that created all things. And thus it is that Paul says: "the invisible things of God from the creation of the world are clearly seen, being understood by the things that are made, even His eternal power and Godhead." Wherefore all the Gentiles knew that there is a God, however much they were Epicureans, however much they maintained that there is no God. Did they not confess God's being in that very denial of Him? For no one can deny that of which he has no knowledge. Wherefore, although men have all their lives long been occupied in the greatest sins and crimes and have lived just as though there were no God, yet they have never been able to cast forth from their minds the conscience that testifies and affirms that God is. And although that conscience has been overborne for a time by evil and perverse opinions yet it comes back to convict them in their life's final breath.'

learned. Or, where resistance is offered to the new teaching, it is yet often noticeably in the face of pressure the other way from the man's own conscience. Such experiences have been made known to me by missionaries among the Tibetans and among African negroes, and it would be interesting to make a collection of them, both in regard to the general question of the *a priori* factors in religion, and especially as throwing light upon the *a priori* knowledge of the essential interdependence of the rational and the non-rational elements in the idea of God. For this the history of religion is itself an almost unanimous witness. Incomplete and defective as the process of moralizing the 'numina' may often have been throughout the wide regions of primitive religious life, everywhere there are traces of it to be found. And wherever religion, escaping from its first crudity of manifestation, has risen to a higher type, this process of synthesis has in all cases set in and continued more and more positively. And this is all the more remarkable when one considers at what widely different dates the imaginative creation of the figures of gods had its rise in different cases, and under what diverse conditions of race, natural endowment, and social and political structure its evolution proceeded. All this points to the existence of *a priori* factors universally and necessarily latent in the human spirit: those, in fact, which we can find directly in our own religious consciousness, when we, too, like Adeimantos, naïvely and spontaneously concur with Socrates' saying, as with an axiom whose truth we have seen for ourselves: 'God is single, and true in deed and word.'

As the rational elements, following *a priori* principles, come together in the historical evolution of religions with the non-rational, they serve to 'schematize' these. This is true, not only in general of the relation of the rational aspect of 'the holy', taken as a whole, to its non-rational, taken as a whole, but also in detail of the several constituent elements of the two aspects. The *tremendum*, the daunting and repelling moment of the numinous, is schematized by means of the rational ideas of justice, moral will, and the exclusion of what is opposed to morality; and schematized thus, it becomes the holy 'wrath of God', which Scripture and Christian preaching alike proclaim.

The *fascinans*, the attracting and alluring moment of the numinous, is schematized by means of the ideas of goodness, mercy, love, and, so schematized, becomes all that we mean by Grace, that term so rich in import, which unites with the holy wrath in a single 'harmony of contrasts', and like it is, from the numinous strain in it, tinged with mysticism. The 'moment' *mysteriosum* is schematized by the *absoluteness* of all rational attributes applied to the Deity. Probably the correspondence here implied – between 'the mysterious' and the *absoluteness* of all rational attributes – will not appear at first sight so immediately evident as in the two foregoing cases, wrath and grace. None the less it is a very exact correspondence. God's rational attributes can be distinguished from like attributes applied to the created spirit by being not relative, as those are, but absolute. Human love is relative, admitting of degrees, and it is the same with human knowledge and human goodness. God's love and knowledge and goodness, on the other hand, and all else that can be asserted of Him in conceptual terms, are formally absolute. The *content* of the attributes is the same; it is an *element of form* which marks them apart as attributes of God. But such an element of form is also the 'mysterious' as such: it is, as we saw on p. 45, the formal aspect of the 'wholly other'. But to this plain correspondence of the two things, 'the mysterious' and the absoluteness of rational attributes, a further one must be added. Our understanding can only compass the relative. That which is in contrast absolute, though it may in a sense be *thought*, cannot be *thought home*, *thought out*; it is within the reach of our conceiving, but it is beyond the grasp of our comprehension. Now, though this does not make what is 'absolute' itself genuinely 'mysterious', as this term was expounded on p. 42, it does make it a genuine *schema* of 'the mysterious'. The absolute exceeds our power to comprehend; the mysterious wholly eludes it. The absolute is that which surpasses the limits of our understanding, not through its actual qualitative character, for that is familiar to us, but through its formal character. The mysterious, on the other hand, is that which lies altogether outside what can be thought, and is, alike in form, quality, and essence, the utterly and 'wholly other'. We see, then, that in the case of the moment of 'mystery', as well as those of 'awefulness' and 'fascination', there is an exact correspondence between the non-rational element and its rational *schema*, and one that admits of development.

By the continual living activity of its non-rational elements a religion is guarded from passing into 'rationalism'. By being steeped in and saturated with rational elements it is guarded from sinking into fanaticism or mere mysticality, or at least from persisting in these, and is qualified to become a religion for all civilized humanity. The degree in which both rational and non-rational elements are jointly present, united in healthy and lovely harmony, affords a criterion to measure the relative rank of religions – and one, too, that is specifically religious. Applying this criterion, we find that Christianity, in this as in other respects, stands out in complete superiority over all its sister religions. The lucid edifice of its clear and pure conceptions, feelings, and experiences is built up on a foundation that goes far deeper than the rational. Yet the non-rational is only the basis, the setting, the woof in the fabric, ever preserving for Christianity its mystical depth, giving religion thereby the deep undertones and heavy shadows of mysticism, without letting it develop into a mere rank growth of mysticality. And thus Christianity, in the healthily proportioned union of its elements, assumes an absolutely classical form and dignity, which is only the more vividly attested in consciousness as we proceed honestly and without prejudice to set it in its place in the comparative study of religions. Then we shall recognize that in Christianity an element of man's spiritual life, which yet has its analogies in other fields, has for the first time come to maturity in a supreme and unparalleled way.

The Manifestations of the 'Holy' and the Faculty of 'Divination'

IT is one thing merely to believe in a reality beyond the senses and another to have experience of it also; it is one thing to have ideas of 'the holy' and another to become consciously aware of it as an operative reality, intervening actively in the phenomenal world. Now it is a fundamental conviction of all religions, of religion as such, we may say, that this latter is possible as well as the former. Religion is convinced not only that the holy and sacred reality is attested by the inward voice of conscience and the religious consciousness, the 'still, small voice' of the Spirit in the heart, by feeling, presentiment, and longing, but also that it may be directly encountered in particular occurrences and events, self-revealed in persons and displayed in actions, in a word, that beside the inner revelation from the Spirit there is an outward revelation of the divine nature. Religious language gives the name of 'sign' to such demonstrative actions and manifestations, in which holiness stands palpably self-revealed. From the time of the most primitive religions everything has counted as a sign that was able to arouse in man the sense of the holy, to excite the feeling of apprehended sanctity, and stimulate it into open activity. Of this kind were those factors and circumstances of which we have already spoken – the thing terrible, sublime, overpowering, or astounding, and in an especial degree the uncomprehended, mysterious thing, which become the 'portent' and 'miracle'. But, as we saw, all these were not 'signs' in the true sense, but opportunities, circumstances, prompting the religious feeling to awake of itself; and the factor promoting this result was found to lie in an element common to them all, but merely analogous with 'the holy'. The interpretation of them as actual appearances of the holy itself in its own nature meant, we saw, a confounding of the category of holiness with something only outwardly resembling it: it was not a genuine '*anamnesis*', a genuine recognition of the holy in its own authentic nature, made manifest in appearance. And therefore we find that such false recognitions of the holy are later rejected and wholly or partly extruded as inadequate or simply unworthy, so soon as a higher level of development and a purer religious judgement have been reached. There is a precisely parallel process in another department of judgement, that of aesthetic taste. While the taste is still crude, a feeling or fore-feeling of the beautiful begins to stir, which must come from an obscure *a priori* conception of beauty already present, else it could not occur at all. The man of crude taste, not being capable of a clear 'recognition' of authentic beauty, falls into confusion and *misapplies* this obscure, dim conception of the beautiful, judging things to be beautiful which are in fact not beautiful at all. Here, as in the case of the judgement of holiness, the principle underlying the erroneous judgement of beauty is one of faint analogy. Certain elements in the thing wrongly judged to be beautiful have a closer or remoter analogy to real beauty. And later here, too, when his taste has been educated, the man rejects with strong aversion the quasi-beautiful but not really beautiful thing and becomes qualified to see and to judge rightly, i.e. to recognize as beautiful the outward object in which the 'beauty' of which he has an inward notion and standard really 'appears'.

Let us call the faculty, of whatever sort it may be, of *genuinely* cognizing and recognizing the holy in its appearances the faculty of *divination*. Does such a faculty exist, and, if so, what is its nature?

To the 'supernaturalistic' theory the matter is simple enough. Divination consists in the fact that a man encounters an occurrence that is not 'natural', in the sense of being inexplicable by the laws of nature. Since it has actually occurred, it must have had a cause; and, since it has no 'natural' cause, it must (so it is said) have a supernatural one. This theory of divination is a genuine, solidly rationalist theory, put together with rigid concepts in a strict demonstrative form and intended as such.

And it claims that the capacity or faculty of divination is the *understanding*, the faculty of reflection in concept and demonstration. The transcendent is here proved as strictly as anything can be proved, logically from given premises.

It would be almost superfluous to adduce in detail in opposition to this view the argument that we have no possibility of establishing that an event did not arise from natural causes or was in conflict with the laws of nature. The religious consciousness itself rises against this desiccation and materialization of what in all religion is surely the most tender and living moment, the actual discovery of and encounter with very deity. Here, if anywhere, coercion by proof and demonstration and the mistaken application of logical and juridical processes should be excluded; here, if anywhere, should be liberty, the unconstrained recognition and inward acknowledgement that comes from deep within the soul, stirred spontaneously, apart from all conceptual theory. If not 'natural science' or 'metaphysics', at least the matured religious consciousness itself spurns such ponderously solid intellectualistic explanations. They are born of rationalism and engender it again; and, as for genuine 'divination', they not only impede it, but despise it as extravagant emotionalism, mysticality, and false romanticism. Genuine divination, in short, has nothing whatever to do with natural law and the relation or lack of relation to it of something experienced. It is not concerned at all with the way in which a phenomenon – be it event, person, or thing – came into existence, but with what it *means*, that is, with its significance as a 'sign' of the holy.

The faculty or capacity of divination appears in the language of dogma hidden beneath the fine name '*testimonium Spiritus Sancti internum*', the inner witness of the Holy Spirit – limited, in the case of dogma, to the recognition of *Scripture* as 'Holy'. And this name is the only right one, and right in a more than figurative sense, when the capacity of divination is itself grasped and appraised by divination. This is not our task here. We therefore employ a psychological rather than a religious expression as being more appropriate to the nature of our discussion.

In this sense, then, 'divination' is no new theological discovery. Schleiermacher, in his *Discourses upon Religion* (1799), Jacob Friedrich Fries, in his doctrine of *Ahndung* ('inkling', surmise, presage), and Schleiermacher's colleague and Fries's pupil, De Wette, have all in effect made use of it and given it a footing in theology, the last-named with special reference to the divination of the divine in history, under the name 'surmise of the divine government of the world'. I have discussed Schleiermacher's discovery at greater length in my edition of his *Discourses*,[1] and in my volume, *Kantisch-Friesische Religionsphilosophie und ihre Anwendung auf die Theologie*, I have given a more precise statement of the *Ahndung* theory, as it is found in Fries and De Wette. To these two works the reader is referred for a more detailed exposition of the matter, and I shall here note only very briefly the more salient features of this doctrine.

What Schleiermacher is feeling after is really the faculty or capacity of deeply absorbed *contemplation*, when confronted by the vast, living totality and reality of things as it is in nature and history. Wherever a mind is exposed in a spirit of absorbed submission to impressions of 'the universe', it becomes capable – so he lays it down – of experiencing 'intuitions' and 'feelings' (*Anschauungen* and *Gefühle*) of something that is, as it were, a sheer overplus, in addition to empirical reality. This overplus, while it cannot be apprehended by mere theoretic cognition of the world and the cosmic system in the form it assumes for science, can nevertheless be really and truly grasped and experienced in *intuition*, and is given form in single 'intuitions'. And these, in turn, assume shape in definite statements and propositions, capable of a certain groping formulation, which are not without analogy with theoretic propositions, but are to be clearly distinguished from them by their free and merely felt, not reasoned, character. In themselves they are groping intimations of meanings figuratively apprehended. They cannot be employed as 'statements of doctrine' in the strict sense, and can neither be built into a system nor used as premisses for theoretical conclusions. But, though these intuitions are limited and

1. Schleiermacher, *Über die Religion.* Göttingen (Vandenhoeck and Ruprecht), pp. 17 ff.

inadequate, they are none the less indisputably *true*, i.e. true as far as they go; and for all Schleiermacher's aversion to the word in this connexion they must certainly be termed *cognitions*, modes of *knowing*, though, of course, not the product of reflection, but the intuitive outcome of feeling. Their import is the glimpse of an Eternal, in and beyond the temporal and penetrating it, the apprehension of a ground and meaning of things in and beyond the empirical and transcending it. They are *surmises* or *inklings* of a Reality fraught with mystery and momentousness. And it is to be noted that Schleiermacher himself sometimes avails himself of the term *ahnden* (divining, surmise) instead of his principal ones, 'intuition' and 'feeling', and expressly connects together the divination of prophecy and the knowledge of 'miracle' in the religious sense of a 'sign'.

When Schleiermacher, in expounding the nature of the experience, tries to elucidate its object by giving examples, he is for the most part led to adduce impressions of a higher τέλος, an ultimate, mysterious, cosmic purposiveness, of which we have a prescient intimation. Here he is quite in agreement with the exposition of Fries, who defines the faculty of *Ahndung* as being just a faculty of divining the 'objective teleology' of the world. And De Wette says the same thing even more unreservedly. But in Schleiermacher this rational element is none the less grounded in eternal mystery, that basis of the cosmos that goes beyond reason. This is shown in the groping, hesitant, tentative manner in which the meaning of the experience always reveals itself. And it is emphasized especially forcibly when Schleiermacher shows where in his own case this experience is to be found in the world he confronts; that it is not so much in its universal conformity to law – a rational quality, interpretable by the intellect in terms of purpose – but rather by means of what appears to us as a baffling 'exception' to law, thereby hinting at a meaning that eludes our understanding.[1]

No intellectual, dialectical dissection or justification of such intuition is possible, nor indeed should any be attempted, for the essence most peculiar to it would only be destroyed thereby. Rather it is once again to aesthetic judgements that we must

1. Op. cit., p. 53.

look for the plainest analogy to it. And the faculty of judging (*Urteilsvermögen*), here presupposed by Schleiermacher, certainly belongs to that 'Judgement' (*Urteilskraft*), which Kant analyses in his Third Critique, and which he himself sets as 'aesthetic judgement' in antithesis to logical judgement. Only, we may not infer from this that the particular several judgements passed in this way need be judgements of 'taste' in their *content*. Kant's distinction between the 'aesthetic' and logical judgement did not mean to imply that the faculty of 'aesthetic' judgement was a judgement upon 'aesthetic' objects in the special narrow sense of the term 'aesthetic', as being concerned with the beautiful. His primary intention is simply and in general terms to separate the faculty of judgement based upon feeling of whatever sort from that of the understanding, from discursive, conceptual thought and inference; and his term 'aesthetic' is simply meant to mark as the peculiarity of the former that, in contrast to logical judgement, it is not worked out in accordance with a clear intellectual scheme, but in conformity to obscure, dim principles which must be felt and cannot be *stated* explicitly as premisses. Kant employs sometimes another expression also to denote such obscure, dim principles of judgement, based on pure feeling, viz. the phrase 'not-unfolded' or 'unexplicated concepts' (*unausgewickelte Begriffe*); and his meaning is here exactly that of the poet, when he says:

> Und wecket der dunklen Gefühle Gewalt,
> Die im Herzen wunderbar schliefen.[1]

Or again:

> Was von Menschen nicht gewusst
> Oder nicht bedacht,
> Durch das Labyrinth der Brust
> Wandelt bei der Nacht.[2]

1. 'It waketh the power of feelings obscure
   That in the heart wondrously slumbered.'
   (SCHILLER: *Der Graf von Habsburg.*)
2. 'What beyond our conscious knowing
   Or our thought's extremest span
   Threads by night the labyrinthine
   Pathways of the breast of man.'
   (GOETHE: *An den Mona.*)

On the other hand, those judgements that spring from pure contemplative feeling also resemble judgements of aesthetic taste in claiming, like them, objective validity, universality, and necessity. The apparently subjective and personal character of the judgement of taste, expressed in the maxim *de gustibus non disputandum*, simply amounts to this, that tastes of different degrees of culture and maturity are first compared, then so opposed one to the other that agreement is impossible. But unanimity, even in judgements of taste, grows and strengthens in the measure in which the taste matures with exercise; so that even here, despite the proverb, there is the possibility of taste being expounded and taught, the possibility of a continually improving appreciation, of convincement and conviction. And if this is true of the judgement arising from aesthetic feeling in the narrower sense, it is at least equally true of the judgement arising from 'contemplation'. Where, on the basis of a real talent in this direction, 'contemplation' grows by careful exercise in depth and inwardness, there what one man feels *can* be 'expounded' and 'brought to consciousness' in another: one man can both educate himself to a genuine and true manner of feeling and be the means of bringing others to the same point; and that is what corresponds in the domain of 'contemplation' to the part played by argument and persuasion in that of logical conviction.

Schleiermacher's exposition of his great discovery suffers from two defects. We will consider one of them here, leaving the other to the next chapter. Schleiermacher, then, naïvely and unreflectingly assumes this faculty or capacity of 'divination' to be a universal one. In point of fact it is not universal if this means that it could be presupposed necessarily in every man of religious conviction as an actual fact, though of course Schleiermacher is quite right in counting it among the general capacities of mind and spirit, and regarding it indeed as the deepest and most peculiar element in mind, and in that sense – man being defined by his intelligent mind – calling it a 'universal human' element. But what is a universal potentiality of man as such is by no means to be found in *actuality* the universal possession of every single man; very frequently it is only

disclosed as a special endowment and equipment of particular gifted individuals. And Schleiermacher gives an excellent
indication of how the matter rightly lies in his very interesting
exposition of the nature and function of the *Mittler* (mediator)
in his first Discourse. Not Man in general (as rationalism holds),
but only special 'divinatory' natures possess the faculty of
divination in actuality; and it is these that receive impressions
of the transcendent, not the undifferentiated aggregate of homo-
geneous individuals in mutual interplay, as held by modern
social psychology.[1]

It is questionable whether Schleiermacher himself, in spite
of his (re-)discovery of 'divination', was a really 'divinatory'
nature, although in his first Discourse he maintains that he
is. One of his contemporaries, to wit, Goethe, was at any rate
decidedly his superior in this respect. In Goethe's life the
power of divination, not latent but finding vital exercise, plays
an important part, and it finds singular expression in the meaning he gives to the term 'daemonic', put with such emphasis in
Dichtung und Wahrheit, Book 20, and in his 'talks' with
Eckermann.[2] Let us briefly examine these. The most characteristic feature in his notion of the 'daemonic' is that it goes
beyond all 'conceiving', surpasses 'understanding' and 'reason',
and consequently is 'inapprehensible' and cannot properly be
put into a statement:

The Daemonic is that which cannot be accounted for by understanding and reason. It chooses for itself obscure times of darkness. . . . In a plain, prosaic town like Berlin it would hardly find
an opportunity to manifest itself. . . . In Poetry there is from first
to last something daemonic, and especially in its unconscious
appeal, for which all intellect and reason is insufficient, and

1. And this is undoubtedly true as far back as the lowest levels of
development, when the 'religious dread' first begins to stir in primitive
form and to manifest itself in ideas. To derive these from an original
group- and mass-fantasy collectively operating is itself sheer fantasy,
and the results this theory helps to produce are about as queer and
grotesque as any of the ideas of which it treats.

2. Cf. Goethe's *Sämtliche Werke*, ed. Cotta, vol. xxv, pp. 124 ff.;
Eckermann, *Gespräche mit Goethe*, ed. A. v. d. Linden, Part II,
pp. 140 ff.

which, therefore, has an efficacy beyond all concepts. Such is the effect in Music in the highest degree, for Music stands too high for any understanding to reach, and an all-mastering efficacy goes forth from it, of which, however, no man is able to give an account. Religious worship cannot therefore do without music. It is one of the foremost means to work upon men with an effect of *marvel*.

'Does not the daemonic (asks Eckermann) also appear in *events*?' 'Pre-eminently so,' said Goethe, 'and assuredly in all which we cannot explain by intellect or reason. And in general it is manifested throughout nature, visible and invisible, in the most diverse ways. Many creatures in the animal kingdom are of a wholly daemonic kind, and in many we see some aspect of the daemonic operative.'

We notice here how the elements of the numinous we discovered plainly recur: the wholly non-rational, incomprehensible by concepts, the elements of mystery, fascination, awefulness, and energy. The note of the daemonic in the animal kingdom reminds us of Job and the leviathan. But in another respect Goethe's intuition falls far short of Job's intuition of the *mysterium*. By his ignoring of the warning of the book of Job and by applying to the *mysterium* the standards of the rational understanding and reason and conceptions of human purpose, the non-rational comes to involve for Goethe a contradiction between meaning and meaninglessness, sense and nonsense, that which promotes and that which frustrates human ends. Sometimes, however, he approximates it to *wisdom*, as when he says:

So there was something daemonic governing the circumstances of my acquaintance with Schiller all through. We might have met earlier or later. But that we should have met just at the time when I had my Italian tour behind me and Schiller had begun to weary of his philosophical speculations – that was a fact of great significance and fraught with success for both of us.

It even comes near the divine:

Such occurrences have often befallen me throughout my life. And one comes in such cases to believe in a higher influence (*Einwirkung*), something daemonic, to which one pays adoration, without presuming to try to explain it further.

Invariably the 'daemonic' has an import of 'energy' and 'overpoweringness', and sets its stamp upon men of vehement and overpowering personality.

'Napoleon', said I, 'seems to have been a daemonic sort of man.'

'He was so absolutely and to such a degree', said Goethe, 'that hardly any other man can be compared with him in this respect. The late Grand Duke also was a daemonic nature, full of limitless, active force and restlessness.'

'Has not Mephistopheles also "daemonic" traits?'

'No, he is much too negative a being. The daemonic manifests itself in a downright positive and active power.'

In *Dichtung und Wahrheit* (p. 126) he delineates still better the impressions such numinous persons make, and in this passage especially sets in the foreground our *tremendum* as the element alike of 'dread' and 'overpoweringness'.

This daemonic character appears in its most *dreadful* form when it stands out dominatingly in some *man*. Such are not always the most remarkable men, either in spiritual quality or natural talents, and they seldom have any goodness of heart to recommend them.[1] But an incredible force goes forth from them and they exercise an incredible power over all creatures, nay, perhaps even over the elements. And who can say how far such an influence may not extend?

But the efficacy and influence of such a 'daemonic' man, even when it is beneficent, moves to amazement rather than to admiration; it is more a tumultuous urgency than ordinary agency, and is at any rate absolutely non-rational. This is what Goethe tries to describe in the series of antitheses in *Dichtung und Wahrheit* (p. 124):

. . . Something that only manifested itself in contradictions and therefore could not be comprehended under any concept, still less under any one word. It was not divine, for it seemed un-reasonable; not human, for it lacked understanding; not devilish, for it was beneficent; not angelic, for it often displayed malicious joy. It was like chance, for it pointed to no consequence; it resembled providence, for it indicated connexion and unity. All

1. i.e. they are merely '*numinous*', not '*holy*' men.

that hems us in seemed penetrable to it; it seemed to dispose at will of the inevitable elements of our being, contracting time and expanding space. Only in the impossible did it seem at home, and the possible it spurned from itself with contempt.

Although this daemonic thing can be manifested in everything corporeal and incorporeal, finding indeed most notable expression among animals, still it is pre-eminently with men that it stands in closest and most wonderful connexion, and there fashions a power which, if not opposed to the moral world order, yet intersects it in such a way that the one might be taken for the warp and the other for the woof.

There can be no clearer expression than this of the prodigiously strong impression which divination of the numinous may make upon the mind, and that obviously not on a single occasion but repeatedly, till it has become almost a matter of habit. But at the same time this 'divination' of Goethe is not one that apprehends the numinous as the prophet does. It does not rise to the elevation of the experience of Job, where the non-rational mystery is at the same time experienced and extolled as supra-rational, as of profoundest *value*, and as holiness in its own right. It is rather the fruit of a mind which, for all its depth, was not equal to such profundities as these, and to which, therefore, the non-rational counterpoint to the melody of life could only sound in confused consonance, not in its authentic harmony, indefinable but palpable. Therefore, though it is genuine divination, it is the divination of Goethe 'the pagan', as he sometimes used to call himself. Indeed, it is a divination that functions only at the level of the 'daemonic' which, as we saw, precedes religion proper, not at the level of the divine and the holy in the truest sense; and it shows very clearly how that sort of merely 'daemonic' experience of the numinous may in a highly cultivated mind only stir emotional reactions of bewilderment and bedazzlement, without giving real light or warmth to the soul. Goethe did not understand how to adjust this divination of the 'daemonic' to his own higher conception of the divine; and, when Eckermann turned the conversation to that, his answer was hesitating and evasive:

'The operative, efficacious force (said I tentatively), which we call the "daemonic", does not seem to fit in with the idea of the divine.' 'Dear boy,' said Goethe, 'what do we know of the idea of the divine, and what can our narrow conceptions presume to tell of the Supreme Being? If I called him by a hundred names, like a Turk, I should yet fall short and have said nothing in comparison to the boundlessness of his attributes.'

But, if we leave out of account the comparatively low level of Goethe's 'divination', we have yet in it a most exact example of what Schleiermacher had in mind. These are 'intuitions and feelings', if not of something divine, still of something numinous in the natural world and in history, and intuitions brought to the higher vitality by an individual with an innate 'divinatory' gift. At the same time the principles on which this divination works cannot even be suggested, for all the examples Goethe may give. What does the 'daemonic' really consist in? How does he come to be conscious of it? How does he identify it as one and the same through all the manifold and contradictory forms in which it manifests itself? These are the questions to which Goethe can suggest no answer. It is evident that in this experience he is being guided by 'mere feeling', that is, by an *a priori* principle that is not explicit and overt, but dim and obscure.

Divination in Primitive Christianity

IN the last chapter we spoke of two defects in Schleiermacher's doctrine of divination. The first of these – his misleading assumption that this is a universal human faculty – has already been considered, and we have now to turn to the second. This is that, though Schleiermacher's description of divination in relation to the world of nature and history has both warmth and insight, he gives no clear detailed account, but only the scantiest hints, of what is after all its worthiest object and the object most propitious to its development, namely, the history of *religion*, especially that of the Bible and its culmination in the person of Christ Himself. His concluding 'discourse' makes emphatic and significant mention of Christianity and Christ, but Christ is here only introduced as the supreme divining *subject*, not as the *object* of divination *par excellence*. And it is the same in Schleiermacher's *Glaubenslehre*. In this, too, the significance of Christ is, essentially, intended to be fully given in the fact that he 'admits us into the power and beatitude of his consciousness of God'. Now this is a thought of high value, but it does not attain to that supreme value which Christianity imputes to Christ, of being in His own person 'holiness made manifest', that is, a person in whose being, life, and mode of living we realize of ourselves by 'intuition and feeling' the self-revealing power and presence of the Godhead. For to the Christian it is a momentous question whether or no a real divination – a direct, first-hand apprehension of holiness manifested, the 'intuition' and 'feeling' of it – can be got from the person and life of Christ; whether, in short, 'the holy' can be independently experienced in Him, making Him a real revelation of it.

In this matter we can obviously get no help from the painful and fundamentally impossible inquiries, so often started, into 'Jesus's consciousness of Himself'. They are impossible, if for no other reason, because the evidence at our disposal is neither sufficient in quantity nor appropriate to such a purpose. Jesus puts as the content of His message and all His utterances, not Himself, but the 'kingdom', its beatitude and righteousness, and, in its first and most straightforward interpretation, the 'gospel' is the 'good tidings' of the kingdom of God. What statements about Himself do occur are fragmentary and incidental. But even were this not the case, even if we could find in the gospels a detailed theory of Jesus as to His own nature, what would this prove? Religious enthusiasts have not infrequently had recourse to the most exalted modes of self-proclamation, and often enough no doubt their statements about themselves have been completely bona fide and sincere. And it is just such self-revealing statements of the prophets of all ages that are more than any others dependent for their form upon their temporal or local context, the equipment of myth or dogma with which his environment supplies the speaker. The fact that the prophet or seer or inspired teacher applies all this material to state something about himself merely demonstrates the intensity of his self-consciousness, his sense of mission, his conviction, and his claim to be believed and obeyed – all of which are to be taken for granted where a man stands forward in response to an inner call. The immediate, intuitive 'divination' of which we are speaking would indeed *not* come as a result of such statements by the prophet about himself, however complete; they can arouse a belief in his authority, but cannot bring about the peculiar experience of spontaneous insight that here is something holy made manifest. 'We have heard him ourselves, and know that this is indeed the Christ' (John iv. 42).

It cannot now be doubted that such an avowal was made of him as a result of a spontaneous, original divination. This must at any rate be true of Christ's own first disciples. Otherwise it would be unintelligible how the Church could have come into existence at all. Mere proclamation, mere authoritative statement, cannot bring about these massive certainties and that impelling strength, that power to maintain and assert itself, which were necessary if the Christian community was to come into being and which can be recognized in it as its unmistakable characteristics.

Misapprehension of this is only possible if, attempting a one-sided approach to the phenomenon of the origin of the Christian Church, we try to reconstruct the facts solely by the methods of scholarship and out of the material afforded by the staled feelings and blunted sensibility of our present-day artificial civilization and complex mentality. It would be an advantage if, in addition to these methods, an attempt were made to frame a less abstract intuition of the genesis of original and genuine religious communities with the aid of living instances of the thing as it may still be found to-day. It would be necessary for this to seek places and moments at which even to-day religion shows itself alive as a naïve emotional force, with all its primal quality of impulse and instinct. This can still be studied in remote corners of the Mohammedan and Indian world. Even to-day one may come upon scenes in the streets of Mogador or Marrakesh, which have the strangest outward resemblance to those recorded by the Synoptic Gospels: 'holy men' (and very queer specimens they generally are!) now and then make their appearance, each the centre of a group of disciples, and about them the people come and go, listening to their sayings, looking at their miracles, observing how they live and what they do. Bands of adherents gather round them, more loosely or more closely united as the case may be. '*Logia*', tales, and legends form and accumulate;[1] new brotherhoods arise or, if already arisen, extend in widening circles. But the centre of it all is always the man himself, a 'holy man' in his lifetime, and what sustains the movement is always the peculiar power of his personality, the special impres-

---

1. It is astonishing that the main problem of Gospel criticism, viz. how the collection of '*Logia*' arose, is not studied in this still-living milieu. It is even more astonishing that the *logia*-series were not long ago elucidated from the closely corresponding milieu of the 'Sayings of the Fathers' ('Aποφθέγματα τῶν Πατέρων), from the Hadith of Muhammed, or from the Franciscan legends. And a particular striking case of the same thing is the collection of the *Logia* of Rāma-Krishna, which has grown to completion in our own day and under our very eyes.

sion he makes on the bystander. Those who should know assure us that ninety-eight per cent of these 'holy men' are impostors; but, even so, we are left with two per cent who are not, a surprisingly high percentage in the case of a matter that invites and facilitates imposture as much as this does. The consideration of this remaining two per cent should continue to throw much light on the actual fact of the genesis of a religious community. The point is that the 'holy man' or the 'prophet' is from the outset, as regards the experience of the circle of his devotees, something more than a 'mere man' ($\psi\iota\lambda\acute{o}\varsigma$ $\ddot{a}\nu\theta\rho\omega\pi\sigma\varsigma$). He is the being of wonder and mystery, who somehow or other is felt to belong to the higher order of things, to the side of the numen itself. It is not that he himself teaches that he is such, but that he is experienced as such. And it is only such experiences, which, while they may be crude enough and result often enough in self-deception, must at least be profoundly and strongly felt, that can give rise to religious communities.

Such cases of contemporary religious movements afford after all a very inadequate analogy, far removed from that which occurred long ago in Palestine. Yet, if even these movements are only made possible by the fact that men actually experience, or presume that they experience, veritable holiness in the personalities of individuals, how far more true must this not be of the early Christian community! That this was so is attested directly by the whole spirit and the universal conviction of the early communities as a whole, so far as we can discern it in their modest records. And certain of the slighter touches in the Synoptic portrait of Jesus confirm the fact expressly in particular cases. We may instance here the narratives already referred to of Peter's haul of fishes (Luke v. 8), and of the centurion of Capernaum (Matt. viii. 8; Luke vii. 6), which point to spontaneous responses of feeling when the holy is directly encountered in experience. Especially apt in this connexion is the passage in Mark x. 32: $\kappa\alpha\grave{\iota}$ $\mathring{\eta}\nu$ $\pi\rho\sigma\acute{a}\gamma\omega\nu$ $\alpha\mathring{\upsilon}\tau\sigma\grave{\upsilon}\varsigma$ $\acute{o}$ $'I\eta\sigma\sigma\mathring{\upsilon}\varsigma\cdot$ $\kappa\alpha\grave{\iota}$ $\mathring{\epsilon}\theta\alpha\mu\beta\sigma\mathring{\upsilon}\nu\tau\sigma$, $\sigma\acute{\iota}$ $\delta\grave{\epsilon}$ $\mathring{a}\kappa\sigma\lambda\sigma\upsilon\theta\sigma\mathring{\upsilon}\nu\tau\epsilon\varsigma$ $\mathring{\epsilon}\phi\sigma\beta\sigma\mathring{\upsilon}\nu\tau\sigma$ ('and Jesus went before them: and they were amazed; and as they followed, they were afraid'). This passage renders with supreme simplicity and force the immediate impression of the numinous that issued from the man Jesus, and no artistry of characterization could do it so powerfully as these few masterly and pregnant words. The later saying in John xx. 28 (the confession of Thomas, 'My Lord and my God') may perhaps appear to us by contrast the utterance of a time too far-reaching in its formulations, and very far removed from the simplicity of the original experience of the disciples. And this passage in Mark may appeal to us all the more just because the living emotion here disdains any precise formulation at all; none the less does it contain the real roots of all later developments of Christology.

Such intimations of the numinous impression made by Jesus upon those who knew Him occur in the Gospel narrative only, as it were, incidentally to the main purpose of the narrator, who is scarcely interested in them, but absorbed rather in the record of the miraculous. In our eyes their interest is all the greater, and we can fancy how numerous similar experiences must have been of which no trace survives in the records, just because there was no miracle to be told of in connexion with them and they were simply taken for granted by the narrator as a matter of course.

To this place belong further the belief in Jesus' supremacy over the demonic world and the tendency to legend that began to take effect from the start; the fact that His own relatives take Him for a man 'possessed', an involuntary acknowledgement of the 'numinous' impression He made upon them; and in an especial degree the conviction that breaks spontaneously upon the minds of His disciples as by a sudden impact, won not from His teaching but from the very experience of Him, that He is the 'Messiah', the being who stood for the circle in which He moved as the numinous being *par excellence*. The experiential character of this belief in His Messiahship stands out clearly in Peter's first confession and Jesus' answer to it (Matt. xvi.15–17): 'Flesh and blood have not revealed it unto thee, but my Father which is in heaven.' Jesus Himself is astonished at Peter's confession, which shows that this was not learnt on authority, but found out by Peter himself, a genuine *discovery*, arising from the impression Jesus made upon him and the testimony borne to it in the depth of the mind, where no teaching of flesh and blood, or even of 'the word', can avail, but only 'my Father in heaven' Himself and without any intermediary.

For this factor – the mind's own witness to the impression – is, it need hardly be said, an indispensable one. Without it all 'impression' is without effect, or rather no impression could occur at all. Therefore, all doctrines of the 'impression made by Christ' are inadequate if they do not pay regard to this second element, which indeed is nothing but the mental predisposition necessary for the experience of holiness, to wit, the category of the holy, potentially present in the spirit as a dim or obscure *a priori* cognition. 'Impress' or 'impression', that is, presupposes something capable of receiving impressions, and that is just what the mind is not, if in itself it is only a 'tabula rasa'. In that richer sense in which we use the word here, we do not in fact mean by 'impression' merely the 'impression' which, in the theory of the Sensationalist school, is the psychical result of sense-perception and is left behind as a psychical trace or vestige of the percept. To be 'impressed' by someone, in the sense we use the term here, means rather to cognize or recognize in him a peculiar significance and to humble oneself before it. And we maintain that this is only possible by an element of cognition, comprehension, and valuation in one's own inner consciousness that goes out to meet the outward presented fact, i.e. by the 'spirit within'. In Schleiermacher's language the 'presentiment' goes out to meet the 'revelation' to which it belongs. Music can only be understood by the musical person; none but he receives an 'impression' of it. And to every unique kind of real impression corresponds in the same way a unique and special sort of 'congeniality', if the word may be used in this special sense of a particular disposition or aptitude, akin to the object arousing the impression. 'Nemo audit verbum, nisi spiritu intus docente.'[1] Once again let us recall the example of the beautiful. A beautiful thing can only make an impression as such, i.e. as signifying beauty, if and in so far as a man possesses in himself *a priori* the potentiality of framing a special standard of valuation, viz. aesthetic valuation. Such a disposition can only be

1. Cf. Luther's remark that only he who is *verbo conformis* understands the Word, and cf. Augustine, *Confessions*, x. 6. 20.

understood as an original, obscure awareness and appreciation of the value of 'beauty' itself. Because a man has this in him, or better, because he is capable of realizing it by training, he is able to recognize beauty in the particular given beautiful object that he encounters, to feel the correspondence of this object with the hidden 'standard of value' within him. And so, and only so, will he get an 'impression'.

CHAPTER XVIII

Divination in Christianity To-day

THE question whether the primitive Church did or could experience holiness in the person of Christ, which we can but answer in the affirmative, is not so important to us as the question whether we too to-day can still do so. Has the portrayal of Christ's life, His actions and achievement, as preserved and handed down by the Christian Church, the value and power of a revelation for us to-day, or do we in this matter but live upon the inheritance bequeathed us by the first community of Christians and base our faith on the authority and testimony of others? There would be no hope of answering this question, were it not that in us too that inner divining power of apprehension and interpretation which has already been considered may find a place – that witness of the spirit, only possible on the basis of a mental predisposition to recognize 'the holy' and to respond to it. If without this no understanding and no 'impression' of Christ was possible even to the first disciples, of what avail should any tradition be that requires the mediation of generations of Christian men? But if we may make this assumption of a predisposing inner 'witness of the Spirit' – as we must – the matter is very different. In that case there is no harm even in the fact that the records of Christ's life are fragmentary, that they contain manifold uncertainties, that they are intermingled with legendary and overlaid with Hellenistic elements. For the Spirit knows and recognizes what is of the Spirit.

As evidence of the way in which this inward principle – this co-witnessing spirit within us – works, prompting, interpreting, and sending out intimation and surmise, I have found the information of a keenly observant missionary from a remote field very instructive. He told me that he had found it a constant matter for fresh astonishment to see how a presentment of the Word so inadequate – which could only hint at its meaning in a difficult foreign tongue and had to work with alien conceptions –

could yet at times win so surprisingly deep and inward an acceptance. And he said that here, too, the best results always were due to the responsive apprehension that came out of the hearer's heart half-way to meet the presented truth. Certainly it is only in this fact that we have a clue to the understanding of the problem of St Paul. Persecutor of the Church as he was, the intimations he had of the being and meaning of Christ and His Gospel must have come to him piecemeal, in fragmentary hints and caricature. But the spirit from within forced upon him the acknowledgement to which he succumbed on the way to Damascus. It taught him that infinitely profound understanding of the Christ made manifest which has led a critic like Wellhausen to confess that, when all is said, no man has understood Christ Himself so deeply and thoroughly as Paul.

If, now, the experience of holiness and 'the holy' in Christ is still to be possible and so afford support to our faith, one thing is evidently to be presupposed at the outset, namely, that His own most immediate and primary achievement and intention can be directly understood and appraised in our experience, so that out of this may grow the 'impression' of His holiness with a like directness. And here a difficulty seems to confront us, which has to be removed if the entire problem is not to be barred from the start. It is this: is that which we to-day think we find in the person of Christ and in Christianity at bottom at all the same as that which He really intended to achieve and that which the first community of His disciples found in Him? In other words, has Christianity really a 'principle' of its own, which, however capable of historical evolution, yet remains unchanged in essence, so that the Christianity of to-day may be measured against the faith of the first disciples and awarded a rank essentially the same?

Is Christianity at all and in a strict sense Jesus' religion? That is, is the religion we know to-day as Christianity, with its peculiar and unique content of belief and feeling, standing in all its historical greatness and supremacy when measured against other religions, with all its power to-day over the hearts and consciences of men to elevate or to excite, to launch accusation or confer benediction, to attract or to repel – is this religion still in its essence and inner meaning the same thing as the simple, unpretentious religion and form of piety which Jesus Himself had, which He Himself aroused and 'founded' in the circle of those little, heart-stirred bands of men in that out-of-the-way corner of the world, Galilee? It must be generally agreed that it has at least changed its form and its colour very significantly since those days, and that it has been exposed to violent alterations and metamorphoses. But is there any abiding essence, any enduring 'principle' at all behind the sequence of its manifestations, susceptible of evolution and development, but remaining one and the same throughout? Is it a case of development and evolution, or rather merely of continual transmutation, the influx of something quite different, which one man laments as a perversion, a second admires as a welcome substitution, and a third merely records as a simple historical fact?

Christianity, as it stands before us to-day in present actuality as a great 'world religion', is indubitably, so far as its claim and promise go, in the first and truest sense a religion of Redemption. Its characteristic ideas to-day are Salvation – overabounding salvation, deliverance from and conquest of the 'world' and from existence in bondage to the world, and even from creaturehood as such, the overcoming of the remoteness of and enmity to God, redemption from servitude to sin and the guilt of sin, reconciliation and atonement, and, in consequence, grace and all the doctrine of grace, the Spirit and the bestowal of the Spirit, the new birth and the new creature. These conceptions are common to Christendom, despite the manifold cleavages that divide it into different confessions, churches, and sects, and they characterize it sharply and definitely as a 'religion of redemption' *par excellence*, setting it in this respect on a level with the great religions of the East, with their sharp, dualistic antithesis of the state of liberation and bondage, nay, justifying its claim not to fall short of these in regard to the necessity of redemption and the grant of salvation, but to surpass them, both in the importance it gives to these conceptions and in the richness of meaning it finds in them. It cannot be doubted that here, in these elements, is to be found the inner 'principle' and essence of contemporary Christianity to-day, and what we have to ask is whether the wealth of mental and emotional content was in very truth the 'principle' of that plain 'religion of Jesus long ago, whose establishment must be termed the first and most immediate achievement of Christ.

In answering this question in the affirmative, we would point to a parable which, intended to have reference to the kingdom of God, fits the principle of Christianity equally well: the parable of the grain of mustard seed and the tree that grew therefrom. This parable hints at a change and alteration, for the grown tree is something different from the seed, but an alteration that is no transformation, no transmutation or 'epigenesis', but genuine 'evolution' or development, the transition from potentiality to actuality.

The 'religion of Jesus' does not change gradually into a religion of redemption; it is in its whole design and tendency a religion of redemption from its earliest commencement, and that in the most uncompromising sense. Though it lacks the theological terms which the Church later possessed, its 'redemptive' character is manifest and unambiguous. If we try to determine as simply and concisely as possible what really characterized the message of Jesus, ignoring what was historically inessential, we are left with two central elements: (1) First, there is the proclamation of *the kingdom of God*, as no mere accessory, but the foundation of the whole Gospel. This is characteristic of His ministry from the beginning and throughout its course. (2) Second, there is the reaction against Pharisaism, and, in connexion with this, Jesus' ideal of godliness as the attitude and mind of a child when its fault has been forgiven. But both points comprise in principle everything which later became separately formulated in the specifically 'redemptive' doctrines of Christianity: Grace, Election, the Holy Ghost, and Renewal by the Spirit. These were possessed by and experienced by that first group of disciples as truly as by any later Christians, though in an implicit form. A closer consideration may make this more plain.

To speak of a 'religion of redemption' is, one may say, to be guilty of a redundancy, at any rate if we are considering the more highly developed forms of religion. For every such religion, when once it has won its autonomy and freed itself from dependent references to an ideal of merely worldly 'welfare' ($\epsilon\dot{v}\delta\alpha\iota\mu\sigma\nu\acute{\iota}\alpha$), whether private or public, develops in itself unique and overabounding ideals of beatitude which may be designated by the general term 'salvation'. Such a 'salvation' is the goal to which the evolution of Indian religions has tended ever more markedly and consciously, from their beginning with the notion of deification of the Upanishad-pantheism on to the bliss-state of the Buddhist Nirvāna, which, as we have seen (p. 53), is negative only in appearance. It is also the goal of the 'religions of redemption', specifically so called, which spread with such vigour over the civilized world from Egypt, Syria, and Asia Minor about the beginning of our era. Further, it is obvious to an examination sharpened by the comparative study of religions that the same tendency to 'salvation' is operative also in the vesture of eschatology that gives form to the religion of Persia. Islam, too, embodies the longing for and the experience of salvation. In this case 'salvation' is not simply in the 'hope' of the joys of Paradise: rather the most vital element in Islam is 'Islam' itself, i.e. that surrender to Allah which is not merely the dedication of the will to Him, but also at the same time the entering upon the 'Allah' state of mind here and now, the object of longing and striving, a frame of mind which *is* already 'salvation', and which may possess and enrapture the man like an intoxication and can give rise to a mystic transport of bliss.

But if the idea of 'salvation' thus lies at the base of all higher religion everywhere, it is manifested quite unmistakably and in supreme fashion, both in intensity and intrinsic purity, in the 'Kingdom of Heaven' of Christianity, which is at once a tenet of faith, an object of desire, and a present experience. It is quite immaterial whether this thought in ancient Israel issued from purely political considerations, only gradually rising above the ground of mere fact, till it finally was exalted to a transcendent meaning, or whether there were from the first authentic religious motives at work to shape and develop it. All this is beside the point, inasmuch as the materials by which the religious impulse works are very frequently at first of an unspiritual, earthly nature. It is just the unresting activity and continual urgency of this impulsion, enabling it to attain to freedom and press onward and upward to ever higher levels of development – it is just this that manifests it most characteristically, and reveals best its inner essential being. And this is nothing else than the pure *impulsion* to *redemption*, and the pre-intimation and anticipation of a boded 'good', transcendent and 'wholly other', a 'salvation' comparable to those 'salvations' striven after in other religions, but supreme above them in the measure in which the Lord of the Kingdom found and possessed in the Christian experience is supreme above Brahmā, Vishnu, Ormuzd, Allah, as also above the Absolute in the form of Nirvāna, Kaivalyam, Tao, or whatever other name it may be given. So redemption is throughout the purport of the gospel even in its first and simplest form, a redemption which is both to be fulfilled by God hereafter and yet at the same time already experienced here and now. In the former aspect it comes as the assured promise of the Kingdom of God; in the latter, by the present experience of His fatherhood, instilled by the Gospel into the soul of the disciple as his most intimate possession. That the early Christians were conscious of this as something entirely novel and unheard of and exceeding all measure (a good *news*), is seen in the saying of Jesus that 'the Law and the Prophets were until John: since that time the kingdom of God is preached' (Luke xvi. 16), in which John the Baptist, who also preached a 'Kingdom of God', is yet classed with 'the Law and the Prophets'.

But to describe this novelty most truly and concisely it would be necessary to *invent* the saying of Paul (Rom. viii. 15), did it not already stand written:

> For ye have not received the spirit of bondage again to fear; but ye have received the Spirit of adoption, whereby we cry, Abba, Father.

Here Paul has penetrated to the heart of the matter, breaking definitely with the older religion and seizing unerringly upon the very principle and essence of the new. And this 'principle and essence' was the same for the first fishermen by the Lake of Galilee and has remained one and the same throughout the whole history of Christianity. With it is given the new attitude to sin and guilt, to law and to freedom, and, *in principle*, 'justification', 'second birth', 'renewal', the bestowal of the Spirit, new creation, and the blissful freedom of God's children. It was inevitable that these or similar expressions and doctrines and the profound speculation to which they would give rise should make their appearance when the Word called to the Spirit responsive to it.[1]

And so Christ's first and direct work and achievement, as we can clearly understand it to-day, is the effectual bestowal of 'salvation' as future hope and present possession by arousing a faith in His God and in the Kingdom of God.

And now how can Divination, in respect to such work of Christ, awake in us also, in us who stand so remote in time from Him? How can we, too, come to experience in Him 'holiness made manifest'?

Obviously not through demonstration and proof, by applying some conceptual rule. We cannot suggest any conceptual criterion in the form: 'When the elements x and y are brought together, a revelation results.' It is just this impossibility which makes us speak of 'divination', 'intuitive apprehension'. The experience must come, not by demonstration, but by pure *contemplation*, through the mind submitting itself unreservedly to a pure 'impression' of the object. For this purpose all that was given and contained in the message and work of Jesus must be combined with the picture of His Person and life and viewed as a whole and in its context with the long and wonderful advance in the religious history of Israel and Judah that was the preparation for it, and with the interplay of diverse tributary lines of development which, even where apparently divergent, ultimately converged upon this as their single culmination. Account must be taken of the elements of 'fulfilment' which the Gospel contains, and due heed given to the attraction and impelling force which it owed to its contrast with its Judaic environment

---

1. We can even comprehend thereby the later influx of 'dualistic' or 'gnostic' currents, or at least see how they became possible. A man like Marcion is an extreme 'Jesu-ist' as well as an extreme 'Paul-ist'.

or to parallels which it bore to this. And all the while, for the full impression to be received, regard is to be paid to the non-rational, the woof of the web, the strange setting of the whole experience, which can nowhere be felt so palpably as in the case of Jesus Christ – how His effect upon the men of His own day rises and ebbs, revealing His spiritual content, on which the salvation of the world depends, ever more and more manifestly, and revealing at the same time that mysteriously growing opposition of powers in which the problem of Job recurs a thousandfold more urgently – where we have the suffering and the defeat not merely of a righteous person, but of all that is most vitally important for the highest interests of humanity. In fine, there is that burden of non-rational, mystical significance, which hangs like a cloud over Golgotha. Whoever can thus immerse himself in contemplation and open his whole mind resolutely to a pure impression of all this combined will surely find growing in him, obedient to an inward standard that defies expression, the pure feeling of 'recognition of holiness', the 'intuition of the eternal in the temporal'. If something eternal, something holy, ever results from the blending and interpenetration of rational and non-rational, purposive and indefinable, elements in the way we tried to describe, in the person of Jesus this stands as nowhere else potently and palpably apparent.

And in a very real sense we of the later day are not worse but more fortunately placed for grasping it than Jesus' own contemporaries. Realization of Him through 'surmise (*Ahndung*) of the divine government of the world'[1] depends essentially upon two factors. On the one hand there is the general view of the marvellous spiritual history of Israel as a connected whole, with its prophetic and religious development, and with Christ appearing as its culmination. And on the other hand there is the complete life-work and achievement of Christ Himself in its entirety. Now in both cases a general comprehensive view is more perfectly to be attained by us to-day than in the time of Christ; for, not only is our historical insight more keen, but we can also see the whole in better perspective at our greater distance. Whoever sinks in contemplation of that great connected

1. An expression of De Wette. (V. p. 164.)

development of the Judaic religion which we speak of as the 'Old Covenant up to Christ' must feel the stirrings of an intimation that something Eternal is there, directing and sustaining it and urging it to its consummation. The impression is simply irresistible. And whoever then goes on to consider how greatly the scene is set for the completion of the whole story and the mighty stature of the personality that is its fulfilment, His firm unfaltering hold upon God, His unwavering, unfailing righteousness, His certitude of conviction and assurance in action so mysterious and profound, His spiritual fervour and beatitude, the struggles and trustfulness, self-surrender and suffering, and finally the conqueror's death that were His — whoever goes on to consider all this must inevitably conclude: 'That is godlike and divine; that is verily Holiness. If there is a God and if He chose to reveal Himself, He could do it no otherwise than thus.'

Such a conclusion is not the result of logical compulsion; it does not follow from clearly conceived premisses; it is an immediate, underivable judgement of pure recognition, and it follows a premiss that defies exposition and springs directly from an irreducible feeling of the truth. But that, as we have seen, is just the manner in which genuine divination, in the sense of an intuition of religious significance, takes place.

Such an intuition, once granted, issues, for us no less than for the first disciples, necessarily and independently of exegesis or the authority of the early Church, in a series of further intuitions respecting the Person, the Work, and the Words of Christ, and it is the task of theology to render these explicit. Such are the intuitions gained of 'sacred history' in general, of its preparation in prophecy, and of its fulfilment in Jesus's 'Messiahship' — the Being in whom all the religious potentialities of prophet and psalmist and all the anticipatory movements and currents in the old covenant became actualized, in whom all previous development found its culmination, and the evolution of a people at once its real significance and its goal, the completion of its course and the consummation of its allotted historical task. And there are further intuitions which have the same origin: the intuition by which we recognize in Christ the portrayal and presentment of God, divining in His agony and victory, His redemptive search and love, the very stamp and signature of God; the intuition of his 'Sonship', by which we recognize Christ as the 'only begotten', the called, the fully empowered with deity, as one whose being, only made possible and intelligible of God, repeats and reveals the divine nature in human fashion; or the intuition of the 'new covenant', of adoption and reconciliation through Christ, of His life-work and self-surrender to God as sacrifice and as a warrant of divine grace. And last, not least, the intuition of the 'covering' and 'propitiating' Mediator. For the abyss between creature and Creator, '*profanum*' and '*sanctum*', sin and holiness, is not diminished but increased by that deeper knowledge that comes from the Gospel of Christ: and, as a result of the emotion spontaneously stirred in the recognition of it, that in which 'the holy' stands self-revealed is taken here, as in other cases, both as the refuge from, and the means by which to approach, Holiness. And this impulsion of the mind to see in Christ mediator and propitiator may be roused to seek expression spontaneously, even in cases where it is not – as in Hebrew and primitive religion – prepared for and sustained by a traditional cult and mysticism of 'sacrifice'. That is, it is a natural religious instinct, due to the pressure of the numinous experience and to nothing else.

We are not, then, to deplore the fact that intuitions of this kind find a place in the doctrines of the Christian faith: they do so of necessity. What we must deplore is, that their free character, as springing from 'divination', is so generally misinterpreted, that too commonly we dogmatize and theorize about them, deducing them from 'necessary truths' of exegesis or dogma (which are in fact always dubious), and so failing to recognize them for what they are, free-floating utterances and trial flights at expression of the numinous feeling; and that too often we give them an emphasis which puts them unwarrantably at the centre of our religious interest, a place which nothing but the experience itself of God ought to occupy.

In this connexion we may draw attention to what are commonly called the 'miracles' of Christ, but which we may perhaps more aptly call, in the words of Mark xvi. 20, 'signs following' (ἐπακολουθοῦντα σημεῖα). It is not upon them primarily that the experience of 'holiness made manifest' is based; but, where there has been real 'divination', there certain traits in the portrait of Christ come to acquire a fresh significance, as confirmation of the divination rather than its ground. I refer to the signs of exalted spiritual power over nature to be detected in the portrait of Jesus. These have their parallels elsewhere in the history of religion: in the great prophets of Israel, for instance, they are shown in the form of that visionary intuition and boding fore-knowledge with which the prophet was endowed for his calling. In the life of Christ they recur unmistakably as 'gifts of the Spirit', raised to a supreme power. These things are not 'mir-acles', for they are powers of the spirit, and so are as 'natural' as our will itself is, with its control over our body. But they clearly only come upon the scene where the spirit is itself exal-ted to its fullest stature and in its fullest vitality, and are most of all to be expected where the spirit is in closest and most in-timate union with its eternal cause and foundation, and is thereby set free to the highest it can itself achieve.

It is, in the last place, clear that it is in the Passion and death of Christ that the objects of the strongest religious intuition must be sought. If His Incarnation, His mission, and the manner of His life come to be considered as a piece of self-revelation, in which an eternal Will of Love is mirrored, before all else is this Love and Faith seen accomplished in the Passion. The Cross becomes in an absolute sense the 'mirror of the eternal Father' (*speculum aeterni Patris*); and not of the 'Father' alone – the highest rational interpretation of the holy – but of Holiness as such. For what makes Christ in a special sense the summary and climax of the course of antecedent religious evolution is pre-eminently this – that in His life, suffering, and death is repeated in classic and absolute form that most mystical of all the problems of the Old Covenant, the problem of *the guiltless suffering of the righteous*, which re-echoes again and again so mys-teriously from Jeremiah and deutero-Isaiah on through Job and the Psalms. The 38th and 39th chapters of Job are a prophecy of Golgotha. And on Golgotha the solution of the problem, already adumbrated in Job, is repeated and surpassed. It lay, as we saw, entirely in the non-rational aspect of deity, and yet was none the less a solution. In Job the suffering of the righteous found its significance as the classic and crucial case of the revelation, more immediately actual and in more palpable proximity than any other, of the transcendent mysteriousness and 'beyondness' of God. The Cross of Christ, that monogram of the eternal mystery, is its completion. Here rational are enfolded with non-rational elements, the revealed commingled with the unrevealed, the most exalted love with the most awe-inspiring 'wrath' of the numen, and therefore, in applying to the Cross of Christ the category 'holy', Christian religious feeling has given birth to a religious intuition profounder and more vital than any to be found in the whole history of religion.

This is what must be borne in mind in the comparison of religions, when we seek to decide which of them is the most perfect. The criterion of the value of a religion as religion cannot ultimately be found in what it has done for culture, nor in its relation to the 'limits of the reason' or the 'limits of humanity' (which, forsooth, are presumed capable of being drawn in advance apart from reference to religion itself!), nor in any of its external features. It can only be found in what is the innermost essence of religion, the idea of holiness as such, and in the degree of perfection with which any given religion realizes this.

There can naturally be no defence of the worth and validity of such religious intuitions of pure feeling that will convince a person who is not prepared to take the religious consciousness itself for granted. Mere general argument, even moral demonstrations, are in this case useless, are indeed for obvious reasons impossible from the outset. On the other hand the criticisms and confutations attempted by such a person are unsound from the start. His weapons are far too short to touch his adversary, for the assailant is always standing right outside the arena! But if these intuitions, these separate responses to the impress upon the spirit of the Gospel story and the central Person of it – if these intuitions are immune from rational criticism, they are equally unaffected by the fluctuating results of Biblical exegesis and the laboured justifications of historical apologetics. For they are possible without these, springing, as they do, from first-hand *personal divination*.[1]

1. Compare with this chapter my book *Reich Gottes und Menschensohn* (*The Kingdom of God and the Son of Man*).

History and the *A Priori* in Religion: Summary and Conclusion

WE have considered 'the holy' on the one hand as an *a priori* category of mind, and on the other as manifesting itself in outward appearance. The contrast here intended is exactly the same as the common contrast of inner and outer, general and special revelation. And if we take 'reason' (*ratio*) as an inclusive term for all cognition which arises in the mind from principles native to it, in contrast to those based upon facts of history, then we may say that the distinction between holiness as an *a priori* category and holiness as revealed in outward appearance is much the same as that between 'reason' (in this wide sense) and history.

Every religion which, so far from being a mere faith in traditional authority, springs from personal assurance and inward convincement (i.e. from an inward first-hand cognition of its truth) – as Christianity does in a unique degree – must presuppose principles in the mind enabling it to be independently recognized as true.[1] But these principles must be *a priori* ones, not to be derived from 'experience' or 'history'. It has little meaning, however edifying it may sound, to say that they are inscribed upon the heart by the pencil of the Holy Spirit 'in history'. For whence comes the assurance that it was the pencil of the 'Holy Spirit' that wrote, and not that of a deceiving spirit of imposture, or of the 'tribal fantasy' of anthropology? Such an assertion is itself a presumption that it is possible to distinguish the signature of the Spirit from others, and thus that we have an *a priori* notion of what is of the Spirit independently of history.

1. The attestation of such principles is the '*testimonium Spiritus Sancti internum*' of which we have already spoken. And this must clearly be itself immediate and self-warranted, else there would be need of another 'witness of the Holy Spirit' to attest the truth of the first, and so on *ad infinitum*.

And there is a further consideration. There is something presupposed by history as such – not only the history of mind or
spirit, with which we are here concerned – which alone makes
it history, and that is the existence of a *quale*, something with a
potentiality of its own, capable of *becoming*, in the special sense
of coming to be that to which it was predisposed and predetermined. An oak-tree can *become*, and thus have a sort of 'history';
whereas a heap of stones cannot. The random addition and sub-
traction, displacement and rearrangement, of elements in a mere
aggregation can certainly be followed in narrative form, but this
is not in the deeper sense an historical narrative. We only have
the history of a people in proportion as it enters upon its course
equipped with an endowment of talents and tendencies; it must
already *be something* if it is really to *become* anything. And biography is a lamentable and unreal business in the case of a man
who has no real unique potentiality of his own, no special idio-
syncrasy, and is therefore a mere point of intersection for various
fortuitous causal series, acted upon, as it were, from without.
Biography is only a real narration of a real life where, by the
interplay of stimulus and experience on the one side and predisposition and natural endowment on the other, something
individual and unique comes into being, which is therefore
neither the result of a 'mere self-unfolding' nor yet the sum
of mere traces and impressions, written from without from
moment to moment upon a *tabula rasa*. In short, to propose a
history of mind is to presuppose a mind or spirit determinately
qualified; to profess to give a history of religion is to presuppose
a spirit specifically qualified for religion.

There are then, three factors in the process by which religion
comes into being in history. First, the interplay of predisposition
and stimulus, which in the historical development of man's
mind actualizes the potentiality in the former, and at the same
time helps to determine its form. Second, the groping recognition, by virtue of this very disposition, of specific portions of
history as the manifestation of 'the holy', with consequent modi-
fication of the religious experience already attained both in its
quality and degree. And third, on the basis of the other two, the
achieved fellowship with 'the holy' in knowing, feeling, and

willing. Plainly, then, religion is only the offspring of history in so far as history on the one hand develops our disposition for knowing the holy, and on the other is itself repeatedly the manifestation of the holy. 'Natural' religion, in contrast to historical, does not exist, and still less does 'innate' religion.[1]

A priori cognitions are not such as everyone does have – such would be *innate* cognitions – but such as everyone is *capable* of having. The loftier *a priori* cognitions are such as – while everyone is indeed capable of having them – do not, as experience teaches us, occur spontaneously, but rather are 'awakened' through the instrumentality of other more highly endowed natures. In relation to these the universal 'predisposition' is merely a faculty of *receptivity* and a *principle of judgement and acknowledgement*, not a capacity to produce the cognitions in question for oneself independently. This latter capacity is confined to those specially 'endowed'. And this 'endowment' is the universal disposition on a higher level and at a higher power, differing from it in quality as well as in degree. The same thing is very evident in the sphere of art: what appears in the multitude as mere receptiveness, the capacity of response and judgement by trained aesthetic taste, reappears at the level of the *artist* as invention, creation, composition, the original production of genius. This difference of level and power, e.g. in musical composition, seen in the contrast between what is a mere capacity for musical experience and the actual production and revelation of music, is obviously something more than a difference of degree. It is very similar in the domain of the religious consciousness, religious production, and revelation. Here, too, most men have only the 'predisposition', in the sense of a receptiveness and susceptibility to religion and a capacity for freely recognizing and judging religious truth at first hand. The 'Spirit' is only 'universal' in the form of the '*testimonium Spiritus internum*' (and this again only '*ubi ipsi visum fuit*'). The higher stage, not to be derived from the first stage of mere receptivity, is in the sphere of religion *the prophet*. The prophet corresponds in the religious sphere to the creative artist in that of art: he is the

1. For the distinction between 'innate' and *a priori* cf. R. Otto. *Religions-philosophie*, p. 42.

man in whom the Spirit shows itself alike as the power to hear the 'voice within' and the power of divination, and in each case appears as a creative force. Yet the prophet does not represent the highest stage. We can think of a third, yet higher, beyond him, a stage of revelation as underivable from that of the prophet as was his from that of common men. We can look, beyond the prophet, to one in whom is found the Spirit in all its plenitude, and who at the same time in His person and in His performance is become most completely the object of divination, in whom Holiness is recognized apparent.

Such a one is more than Prophet. He is the Son.

The Expression of the Numinous in English[1]

ALTHOUGH it could hardly be disputed that the German philosophical vocabulary is superior to the English both in fullness and in precision, in regard to the subjects discussed in this book our language does not seem to be altogether at a disadvantage. Indeed, the English wealth of synonyms has presented the translator with an embarrassment at the very outset. In place of the single German adjective *heilig*, with its derivative noun and verb, we have the words *sacred* and *holy*, *sacredness*, *holiness*, and *sanctity*, *hallow* and *sanctify*. *Gottheit* again gives us a triad of synonyms, *deity*, *divinity*, *Godhead*. Each of these alternatives is probably the most appropriate rendering in some special context, and in choosing any one of them we are bound to sacrifice subtle differences in meaning which would be suggested by the others, and which are perhaps implicit in the single German equivalent. The deciding factor in the choice of *holy* rather than *sacred* as the regular rendering of *heilig* was the fact that it is the Biblical word, found especially in those great passages (e.g. Isa. vi) of which this book makes repeated use, and which seem central to its argument. *Holy* will be felt, I believe, to be a distinctly more numinous word than *sacred*: it retains about it more markedly the numinous atmosphere. And although, as is urged in the text with perhaps still more reason of its German equivalent, it refers mainly to the higher levels of religious experience at which the numinous has been interpreted in rational and moral terms, and therefore means to us mainly *goodness*, the word 'holy' is found also in contexts where this more exalted meaning is excluded, and where it is simply the numinous at an early and savage stage of development. The well-known lines from Coleridge's *Kubla Khan* give an example of such a use:

> A savage place! as holy and enchanted
> As e'er beneath a waning moon was haunted
> By woman wailing for her demon-lover!

1. Added by the translator.

This is a finely numinous passage, but it is the numinous at the primitive, pre-religious, 'daemonic' level: it conveys nothing of sanctity. For, while the daring use of 'holy' in this context may be just permissible, we reserve 'sanctity', if I mistake not, for the more restricted and elevated meaning.

Apart from these words it would appear that the English language is in general rich in numinous terms. Dr Otto has himself noted (p. 28) that the English 'awe' has a numinous suggestion lacking in the German *scheu*, and (p. 144*n*.) that 'haunt' has no precise German equivalent in all its range of significance. And besides 'uncanny' (a more or less exact rendering of *unheimlich*) I have made use of words like *weird* and *eerie*, which convey the indefinable numinous atmosphere unmistakably. The old word *freit* (a supernatural intimation or sign) may be another such; and possibly the obsolete verb-form *oug*, which gives us *ugly*, may have conveyed originally a suggestion of unnatural, uncanny daunting or repulsion. It should be noticed that these numinous words are all (except 'awe') concerned *primarily* with the cruder and more primitive forms of the experience: they are not in the first instance *religious* words in the higher sense, though, unlike such words as *grue*, *grisly*, and *ghastly*, they can be used with a loftier and more ennobled, as well as with a lower and more primitive meaning. And it can, finally, be hardly an accident that they all, or nearly all, are northern in origin. A peculiar susceptibility to numinous impressions – what Dr Otto would call a peculiarly sensitive faculty of 'divination' – would seem, indeed, to be a characteristic of the North British. Such phenomena as those of clairvoyance and second-sight would seem to make for the same conclusion.

Apart from the expressiveness of single English words, it would be easy to amass from English poetry and prose alike passages (like that from Coleridge already quoted) illustrative of the different elements in numinous apprehension which have been discussed in this book. I venture to give two further citations.

The same antithesis could hardly be shown more clearly than by the contrast between two poems familiar to every English reader, Addison's hymn based on Ps. xix, and Blake's poem 'The Tyger'. Both poets are hymning the Creator as revealed in His creation, but the difference of temper is unmistakable. On the one hand there is the mood of tranquil confidence, serene dignity, thankful and understanding praise; on the other, a mood of trepidation, awed surmise, the hush of mystery, in which rings none the less a strange exultation.

> The spacious firmament on high
> With all the blue ethereal sky,
> And spangled heavens, a shining frame,
> Their great Original proclaim.
> The unwearied sun, from day to day,
> Does his Creator's power display
> And publishes to every land
> The work of an Almighty hand.
>
> Soon as the evening shades prevail
> The moon takes up the wondrous tale
> And nightly to the listening earth
> Repeats the story of her birth;
> While all the stars that round her burn,
> And all the planets in their turn,
> Confirm the tidings as they roll
> And spread the truth from pole to pole.
>
> What though in solemn silence all
> Move round the dark terrestrial ball;
> What though no real voice or sound
> Amid their radiant orbs be found?
> In reason's ear they all rejoice,
> And utter forth a glorious voice;
> For ever singing as they shine:
> 'The hand that made us is Divine'.

This is, confessedly, *rational* piety; it is 'reason' that listens to nature's hymn of praise. As such it is characteristic not only of a certain type of mind, but of the particular age in which it was written. And the contrasted numinous note can hardly be missed in Blake's wonderful verses:

> Tyger, Tyger, burning bright
> In the forests of the night,
> What immortal hand or eye
> Could frame thy fearful symmetry?
>
> In what distant deeps or skies
> Burnt the fire of thine eyes?
> On what wings dare he aspire?
> What the hand dare seize the fire?

And what shoulder and what art
Could twist the sinews of thy heart?
And, when thy heart began to beat,
What dread hand and what dread feet?

What the hammer? What the chain?
In what furnace was thy brain?
What the anvil? What dread grasp
Dare its deadly terrors clasp?

When the stars threw down their spears,
And watered heaven with their tears,
Did He smile His work to see?
Did He who made the lamb make thee?

Tyger, Tyger, burning bright
In the forests of the night,
What immortal hand or eye
Dare frame thy fearful symmetry?

My last quotation comes from Wordsworth. In the tenth book of *The Prelude*, he recounts the profound impression made upon him by the terrific events in which the French Revolution culminated. Then, as now, outward convulsion and catastrophe had their inward counterpart in spiritual tumult and overthrow, in widespread disillusionment and despair. And Wordsworth tells us in effect how the very tremendousness of the time, its 'portentousness', became to him a revelation of the sustaining presence of the holy and the divine (see *The Prelude*, x. 437–69):

    . . . 'So, with devout humility be it said,
So, did a portion of that spirit fall
On me uplifted from the vantage-ground
Of pity and sorrow to a state of being
That through the time's exceeding fierceness saw
Glimpses of retribution, terrible,
And in the order of sublime behests:
But, even if that were not, amid the awe
Of unintelligible chastisement,
Not only acquiescences of faith
Survived, but daring sympathies with power,
Motions not treacherous or profane, else why

The Idea of the Holy

Within the folds of no ungentle breast
Their dread vibration to this hour prolonged? . . .
Then was the truth received into my heart,
That, under heaviest sorrow earth can bring,
If from the affliction somewhere do not grow
Honour which could not else have been, a faith,
An elevation, and a sanctity,
If new strength be not given nor old restored,
The blame is ours, not Nature's.

Index

Index

Index